STUDYING
YOUR
WORKFORCE

*To William M. Rivera, Jr., teacher, advisor, and mentor,
who showed me how the world of the intellect can be
applied in service to the practical benefit of others.*

STUDYING YOUR WORKFORCE

Applied Research
Methods and
Tools for the
Training and
Development
Practitioner

Alan Clardy

SAGE Publications
International Educational and Professional Publisher
Thousand Oaks   London   New Delhi

For information:

SAGE Publications, Inc.
2455 Teller Road
Thousand Oaks, California 91320
E-mail: order@sagepub.com

SAGE Publications Ltd.
6 Bonhill Street
London EC2A 4PU
United Kingdom

SAGE Publications India Pvt. Ltd.
M-32 Market
Greater Kailash I
New Delhi 110 048 India

Printed in the United States of America

Library of Congress Cataloging-in-Publication Data

Clardy, Alan
   Studying your workforce : applied research methods and tools for
the training and development practitioner / Alan Clardy.
      p.   cm.
   Includes bibliographical references and index.
   ISBN 0-8039-7321-7 (acid-free paper). — ISBN 0-8039-7322-5 (pbk.:
   acid-free paper)
      1. Personnel management—Research—Methodology. 2. Employees—
   Training of—Evaluation. I. Title.
   HF5549.15.C575 1997
   658.3'124'072—dc21   97-4672

This book is printed on acid-free paper.

97 98 99 00 01 02 03 10 9 8 7 6 5 4 3 2 1

Acquiring Editor:	Marquita Flemming
Editorial Assistant:	Frances Borghi
Production Editor:	Sherrise M. Purdum
Production Assistant:	Karen Wiley
Typesetter/Designer:	Danielle Dillahunt
Cover Designer:	Lesa Valdez
Print Buyer:	Anna Chin

CONTENTS

■

TABLES, FIGURES, CHARTS, EXHIBITS

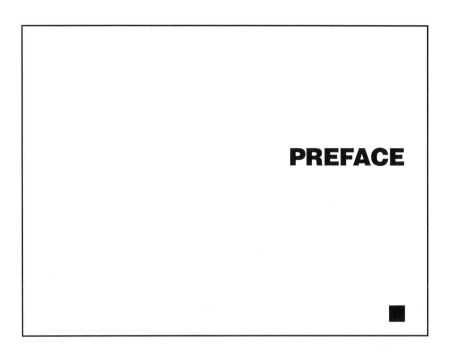

PREFACE

This book is intended to provide an introduction to the issues, methods, and tools of research as they should be applied to the process of training an organization's human resources. The book is written for the training practitioner with limited, if any, training or education in social or behavioral science; it could equally be helpful as a review for those people who took a basic survey course in research techniques as an undergraduate years earlier. Thus, this book assumes that the reader has little, if any, background in social and behavioral science research.

Moreover, this book does *not* require that the reader be conversant in statistics, nor does it cover statistical methods of analysis. Indeed, a derivative message of this book is that, other than basic skills in calculating percents, forming tables, and the like, much of the applied research in which most human resources development practitioners will find themselves engaged can be completed *without* relying on sophisticated statistical methods or techniques. This is not to excuse practitioners from becoming familiar with statistics and elevating their practice with more refined methods; it is simply to say that basic applied training research does not require an intermediate-level mastery of statistics.

The book is designed to provide practical, step-by-step guidance in how to conduct meaningful and useful research to support human resources development (HRD) programming. To do this, research activities have been divided into three principal stages of training practice. Since training is positioned as a means of addressing performance problems in organized work settings, each stage of research revolves around the issues of detecting, affecting, and assessing performance problems. The first stage of the training process supported through research involves identifying performance problems to establish the need and direction for any subsequent training. The second stage of training involves using research to develop and implement training-based solutions to performance problems. Research for the third stage of training practice involves evaluating the adequacy and value of the human resources development solutions used to solve the performance issues raised in stage one.

■ Plan of the Book

This volume is organized to lead the reader through a discussion of how research can be applied to human resources development. Chapter 1 considers the importance of training and employee development in today's workplace. On this foundation is erected an argument for the benefits of applied research. The distinctive features of applied research are contrasted with the traditional principles of theoretically oriented science. The training process is presented as a three-stage model, and the ways research is linked to each stage are described.

Chapters 2 and 3 cover the nuts and bolts of research methods, the "how to" of data collection. Four principal methods of primary data collection—tests, observation, survey questionnaires, and interviewing—are reviewed, along with special applications of each. These two chapters summarize the mechanics of data collection usually covered in more traditional research methodology texts. The summaries are intended to provide simple guidelines and procedures for implementing each technique as circumstances may dictate. Readers familiar with the mechanics of data collection may wish to skim or skip these chapters.

The remaining chapters of the book turn attention from the *how* to the *what* of data collection. That is, these chapters focus on what kind of information should be collected as part of a HRD program. For example, Chapters 4 and 5 examine different methods for identifying and analyzing performance problems. This stage of applied training research is usually called "needs assessment," a catchall term found wanting and replaced by the more adequate concept of "front-end assessment." Four distinctive yet related types of front-end assessment are examined. Chapter 6 looks at what kind of information research should collect to help develop and implement training-based solutions to performance problems. Again, several different kinds of research applications are discussed.

Finally, Chapter 7 describes the types of issues involved with, and procedures for, evaluating HRD programs. After several approaches to evaluation are considered, a general set of guidelines for conducting an assessment of a training program is outlined.

■ Thanks and Exemptions

This book emerges from a course I developed and taught as part of Towson State University's master's degree program in Human Resources Development. The book demonstrates how I have tried to translate and interpret the mandates, strictures, and lessons of classic scientific research and the canons of training and development into terms and procedures that are relevant to those grappling daily with human performance problems in their organizations. I would like to thank Dr. Larry Froman, the program director at Towson State, for recognizing the need for a new course in the curriculum on basic research methods applied to HRD and for asking me to take that challenge. The students also need to be thanked for their assistance in sitting through and reacting to presentations of materials that may have seemed either alien, disjointed, or both. To them, there may be small comfort in knowing that their travail did bear fruit in what I believe is now a clearer and more accessible approach to research applied to human resources development. I also want to thank Larry, Cindy Larson of the Baltimore Federal Reserve, Margaret Baldwin of Cadmus, an anonymous reviewer, and Marquita Flemming of Sage for their helpful comments, suggestions, and remarks. Marquita deserves special praise for being patient in waiting out the oft-promised yet chronically late submission of the manuscript. They should be excused from any of the boneheaded errors stubbornly resisting dismissal from the body of this work.

ALAN CLARDY

1

USING RESEARCH
FOR TRAINING
AND DEVELOPMENT

■

Several years ago, after 20 years' experience in the field of human resources and training and by which time I surely should have known better, I goofed. I was working on a consulting project with a community bank to revise its performance appraisal system and then train its management staff how to use it. The planning and revision of the performance appraisal procedure went very well, and the task force of 10 or so managers working with me on the project were pleased with the new process. Since employee appraisal was one of my specialty areas, I thought it would be possible to use my basic appraisal training package with this group. But a good procedure and a basic training package does not an effective training program make, as I discovered early on in the training, when previously earned laurels were quickly knocked off my head.

Flashback to the negotiations for doing this project: During those discussions, the bank made it clear that its budget was limited, and it declined any needs assessment of the trainees. I neither factored in any pilot testing of the training program for this group nor assessed any of the entry characteristics of the trainees (such as amount of training background in the topic or their motivation). Given the budget regimen, it should come as no surprise that there was no plan for program evaluation, either. As it turned out, both the bank and I had been the proverbial penny-wise and pound-foolish.

Fast-forward to the training: An early indication of training problems occurred when the president of the bank appeared at the start of the program only to leave during the first hour. His departure triggered a process of incremental attrition that meant slow death to the training, as a few more participants left at every break, group exercise, or new section to be covered. Less than half of the 25 initial participants returned from lunch, and the director of Human Resources coordinating the program and I decided to cut the program short. It was a disaster.

What happened? Having carried out the same basic program at other financial institutions with some degree of success, I felt the problem was not inherently or entirely due to me or the program itself. Rather, the successful application of the training to this group of trainees failed across a variety of fronts, and the immediate cause of these failures was a lack of research in the planning, design, and evaluation of the training program. Better research at each stage would have led me to anticipate some potential problems, allowing better adaptation of the training to the group to be trained and permitting better assessment of the value of the training. During the contracting phase of the engagement, I did not appreciate this principle, and the results suffered.

Beyond the immediate research problem, there was also a more fundamental, underlying issue: the lack of client management support and commitment to develop and implement a complete HRD program. As discussed more fully in the following pages and in Chapter 3, client managers tend to want quick, easy fixes to their performance problems. Research activities add time and cost without any obvious gains in the program. Thus, in addition to not undertaking the necessary research in program planning and development, I also failed to explain why research was necessary. This lesson should not be lost: Not only should training practitioners be skilled in carrying out necessary program research, but they should also be ready and able to articulate the reasons why such research is a vital and essential step along the way.

■ Research and
Human Resources Development

Human resources development (HRD) is a process for helping employees learn how to perform their current or future jobs more effectively. Although this mission seems straightforward enough, the route to its accomplishment can be tricky, for along the way a number of questions arise about planning, developing, and evaluating HRD activities: What kind of training is needed? What kinds of learning activities should be used? Did the program work?

In this volume, *research* is understood to refer to the systematic and controlled process of collecting and analyzing information necessary or useful to the efficient and effective provision of HRD programs. Research involves discovering the information needed to answer these basic questions, and as such, research becomes the essential handmaiden of effective HRD practice. When speaking of research, however, the image of experimental, theoretically driven scientific methods and procedures—men and women in lab coats with clipboards—is conjured up. Although the methods and procedures of science have much to teach the HRD practitioner about research procedures and techniques, classical science is *not* the appropriate model for conducting applied HRD research.

In this chapter, some of the typical problems and concerns to which HRD efforts may be applied will be noted, along with the role research plays in dealing with such problems. HRD will then be defined in the context of a variety of related disciplines and fields available to the practitioner for influencing human performance in work settings. Reasons why research is so important to the effective execution of HRD projects will be presented. Given the growing role that HRD is expected to play in developing a world-class workforce, gaining support for applied research becomes even more critical. The characteristics of applied HRD research will be reviewed in comparison with the traditional approach of theoretically oriented science. Finally, this chapter will outline the model of HRD research presented in this book.

■ Typical HRD Research Problems

My first job in HRD involved finishing up an evaluation of a management training program. The 3-day program was offered to groups of hospital laboratory managers; 10 such programs had been given at different regional centers, and at the conclusion of each, participants filled out an evaluation of the program. The evaluation asked for their opinions of the program, how much they liked it, how well it was conducted, and so forth. The ostensible purpose of the evaluation was to provide to the agency funding the training a judgment about the adequacy or effectiveness of the training. Not until later, after more experience and more study, did I realize how inadequate—but typical—the evaluation process was. But this project taught me the importance of sound research practices to the skillful and effective execution of HRD programs.

Indeed, in over 25 years of working in all aspects of HRD and management, I have been involved in a number of research projects related to the management and development of managers, employees, volunteers, and customers. The following list of some of the problems on which I've worked suggests the range of research projects that may face the HRD practitioner.

1. *Assessing workforce attitudes and satisfaction.* Faced with growing employee discontent sparked by what the employees perceived to be an insufficient raise, a municipal government wanted to learn about the nature, focus, extent, and severity of that discontent. I drew up and administered a special opinion survey to assess employee satisfaction, then analyzed and reported the results to the city manager's staff.

2. *Studying reasons for turnover and poor transfer of training.* While I was managing a training department for a large bank, it was important to learn the reasons why some tellers did very well and others struggled after completing a 3-week training program. Those who faced the most difficulty were the ones most likely to quit soon after the training was finished. A study comparing a cohort of recent trainees was conducted to identify ways to address the reasons why the formal training did not transfer back to the job and the subsequent poor performance experienced by some tellers.

3. *Designing a new training program.* Also at the bank, a new program for training head tellers was planned. To design the training program, we surveyed head tellers to identify the tasks they performed and discover which of those areas would benefit from training.

4. *Identifying specific training needs.* A large regional credit union had adopted a performance appraisal system 2 years earlier. Annually, managers attended refresher training, a habit the credit union wished to continue. To find out what kind of training, if any, the managers should obtain in the third year, an extensive needs assessment was conducted that included a survey of appraisal practices used (parallel forms sent to both managers and their employees), a review of the appraisal forms sent in the year before, and a simulated appraisal discussion that was videotaped and then analyzed.

5. *Identifying improvements to human resources programs.* In my recent consulting assignments, focus groups of managers and supervisors were put together to critique the organization's existing performance management system and suggest improvements as part of a reeingineering effort.

6. *Promoting changes in manager practices.* To encourage the adoption of a new performance management and appraisal system at a small community bank, a survey form for gathering employee assessments of and satisfaction with the current level of feedback they received from their managers was developed and

administered. Results of the survey, which showed that employees wanted but did not receive adequate performance feedback from their supervisors, were shared with the managers attending the training.

7. *Manpower and succession planning.* A small financial institution, knowing of the imminent retirement of its two top executives, needed to know about the depth of its management team to prepare for executive succession. The bank's market position and business plan were studied to isolate critical management skills and then each member of the management team was assessed against those criteria to identify strengths and developmental needs. A plan for managing the succession process was prepared.

8. *Training program evaluation.* Based on the employee satisfaction survey mentioned earlier (1), the management staff of the municipal government attended a supervisory development program. All front-line supervisors attended one program and mid-managers attended another. About halfway through the 8-week program, complaints from the management group led to a program review to determine whether the program needed to be modified or stopped. I designed a survey to gather opinions and interviewed the participants. The information collected was used to make a final decision about the disposition of the program. (It was stopped.)

In all of these cases, new and specific information had to be collected about a specific human resources problem, program, or opportunity. The results of this research were used to identify HRD needs, plan for and develop HRD programs, and evaluate HRD efforts. These examples illustrate how research is essential to the effective execution of HRD practices. The range of activities covered begs the question, however, of what *human resources development* is.

■ HRD: Defining the Field

A number of academic and applied fields of interest share a common goal of influencing human performance in organized work settings to achieve optimum results in productivity, quality of life, and organizational effectiveness. These fields include the various domains of human resources management (HRM), such as compensation and selection, organizational behavior, organization or human systems development (Tannenbaum, Marguiles, Massarik, & Associates, 1987), total quality management (TQM), action research, instructional systems design, reengineering, and HRD. With the possible exception of organizational behavior, all of these disciplines tend to have an applied orientation. That is, these fields focus more on how to use knowledge and techniques to address concrete, everyday problems of human performance than on how to abstract phenomena into theories and to test the hypotheses derived from these theories. Although each discipline has its own distinctive approaches for gathering, interpreting and applying information, there is much that these disciplines share. For example, HRM programs, organization development, TQM, and reengineering all tend to be passed into a workplace and given operational life through some kind of training program.

Performance and Training

Human performance in work settings is a function of the motivation and abilities of the people involved and the opportunities and constraints imposed by the social system in which they must perform. This relationship is often referred to as the *performance equation* (Blumberg & Pringle, 1982). Each of the disciplines previously noted focuses on some or all aspects of this performance equation. For example, instructional systems design (ISD) considers all aspects of this equation from the view of what factors may be inhibiting effective performance (Rothwell & Kazanas, 1992). Training, or HRD (for ease of exposition, the terms will be used synonymously in this book), finds its niche in this panoply of applied fields by concentrating on the abilities component of the equation. Here, *human resources development* (HRD) will be defined as a formal process of helping employees learn the skills and abilities they need to perform their jobs, either now or in the future. Note that this definition does not limit attention to only formal classroom programs: Any planned or structured learning process can be gathered under the HRD wing. Brinkerhoff and Gill (1994), casting HRD as a performance improvement system, put it this way:

> In performance improvement systems, the core service is learning. Learning is the primary result of training interventions, be they seminars, self-instructional packages, workshops, on-the-job training sessions, or mentoring. However, learning alone adds little value. . . . Improved job performance comes when learning interventions, the core service of training, are integrated within a larger set of value-adding services. (p. 114)

One should be careful, however, not to draw lines between these disciplines that are too deep or bold. As already noted, these disciplines share much in common, including the application of research to the problems of human performance in work settings. Although this book will examine the mechanics of the research process from a HRD point of view, the core methods and techniques covered here can easily be extended to the other fields.

■ The Importance of Research to Effective HRD Practice

The Hoopla About Training

A competent and committed workforce is increasingly being seen as a key to building a firm's competitive advantage, and the efficient, effective provision of HRD services is being seen as an essential element in developing "competitive advantage through people" (Pfeffer, 1994). To meet these expectations, the HRD practitioner must be skilled in gathering, analyzing, and using information in the planning, design, and evaluation of training programs. Without good research behind such programming, the customer does not receive the best value.

Any applied profession can be defined, in part, as the application of a research methodology to diagnose, treat, and solve the real-world problems bounded by the discipline. Regardless of whether those problems involve group process, production quality, or employee skill proficiency, the applied profession depends on using certain research practices to undertake and complete its mission. In other words, the hallmark of an applied profession is researching certain problems so that appropriate ministrations can be applied. In the disciplines just noted, ministrations are often called *interventions* and include such activities as team building, training programs, or job analysis and evaluation. To be an effective practitioner in any of these disciplines, one must be properly trained and skilled in carrying out applied research. Effective HRD programs should be built on a sound research foundation.

Although these points have always been true, the importance of research to HRD has been rising. There are three reasons why well-conducted, applied research is increasingly critical to the successful achievement of the HRD mission. First, there is a growing interest in accountability brought about by the sheer size and scope of training activity. The total estimated training budget for firms in the United States with 100 or more employees was estimated to be more than $50 billion in 1995 ("1995 Industry Report," 1995). Even in firms with 100 to 500 employees, training budgets averaged more than $125,000 during this same period. Training expenditures now involve significant money, but with notoriety comes closer scrutiny, particularly in periods of cost-cutting and downsizing. What does the organization get for its training budget? What benefits does the organization reap from its training expenditures? To command scarce budget dollars, training must be accountable, and evaluation research is essential for addressing this issue.

Second, in addition to the size and scope of training, there is a second factor: the increasing requirement that training contribute to organizational performance. Charles Fay (1990) paints the background scenery in this way:

> The United States, with its high standard of living and high worker expectations, can compete with organizations in other countries only by maintaining higher levels of productivity. . . . If American organizations are to remain competitive, they must harness the energies of their employees to work toward higher levels of productivity. In many cases, this does not necessarily mean that employees need to work harder. (p. 346)

More effort can only go so far. Working smarter is critical to building and sustaining competitive advantage, and training becomes an essential vehicle for developing the smarter and more effective application of talent.

Regardless of the size of the training budget, training is expected to deliver results. In Kling's (1995) review of high-performance systems research, for example, training is singled out as the largest contributor to superior firm performance, compared to incentive and employee involvement programs. Many firms, large and small, find themselves operating under intense market conditions, characterized by a number of competitors all chasing a limited customer base. Workers unprepared to satisfy customer needs represent a potential loss of business and market share. Furthermore, when global competitors with lower production costs are added into the mix, even the best service may not offset price advantages. Poor productivity can then double the firm's woes.

Training is a principal method for warding off employee service and productivity problems—but only if the training works. Research is an essential step in planning and preparing HRD programs that deliver. Research is critical for assessing the kind of specific training that is needed and for designing a training program with the best potential to achieve the desired results. Off-the-shelf, canned HRD programs cannot be counted on to yield the results demanded by today's workplace.

The third factor that is increasing the role of research in HRD practice is strategic alignment (Rothwell & Kazanas, 1989). Not only should HRD be held accountable for its effect on current performance, HRD should also support the longer-term strategic direction of the organization. Strategy directs what the organization should be doing in the years ahead, and HRD programs should support that direction. Research helps establish what specific HRD programs and practices are needed to support an organization's strategic movement (Schneider & Konz, 1989).

In general, then, the marginal costs of applying research to an HRD program are easily offset by the savings and returns that the research adds to the overall value of the program. In short, appropriate research applied to HRD problems and programs should yield the following benefits.

1. By identifying the projects and conditions that represent high-value gains to the organization, research increases the effect of the training dollars, yielding a better return on training resources consumed. HRD programming is often noted for its faddishness, bringing in the latest program (e.g., time management, reengineering, or empowerment) because it seems "hot." But value comes from working on those areas that are critical to success and on which performance is lagging. The methods of organizational assessment reviewed in Chapter 4 will show how to identify and isolate high-value HRD opportunities.

2. By discovering the most prevalent causes of a performance problem—for example, lack of skill, poor motivation, or inefficient work systems—better results can be obtained more quickly, increasing productivity and customer satisfaction in the process. Line managers are typically known to call for training whenever there is a problem. Yet there may be causes for the performance problem other than lack of knowledge and skills. In such situations, HRD may at best provide a partial solution and, at worst, waste time and resources following a proverbial wild goose. Approaches for determining the causes of performance problems are discussed in Chapter 5.

3. By carefully detailing the tasks for which training is required and by screening program participants in terms of their relative training needs and commitments, wasted time and expense can be avoided. Ask trainers how many times they have had to conduct a program that included people who didn't need to be there (already skilled) or shouldn't have been there (bad attitude), and the answer will probably be "a lot." Chapters 5 and 6 suggest ways that research can help overcome these issues.

4. By developing learning procedures and activities that are best suited to the specific needs of participants, more learning can occur, which in turn paves the way for better application of the newly learned talents on the job. An important principle in promoting the transfer of training is to make the training conditions as similar as possible to the real-world job performance conditions. In addition, training fidelity to the real world can increase learner attention and recognition of instructional materials. Research can help determine critical features of the real world that should be adapted to the HRD initiative; such techniques will be explored in Chapter 6.

5. By assessing how well training is working, better decisions can be made with regard to allocating limited financial, temporal, and management resources and determining whether to continue, modify, or stop the HRD programs. In the example mentioned earlier, after studying what was happening with a management training program, the decision was made to conserve remaining budget dollars and staff time by stopping the program. In other cases, learning that a program is

working well might suggest devoting more resources to it. Chapter 7 looks at these evaluation issues.

For all of these benefits to follow from HRD research, the appropriate kind of research must be done—and done well. We turn next to the question of what kind of research model is appropriate for HRD.

■ HRD Research and the Scientific Method

Typically, the research training that HRD practitioners receive is provided in anticipation of a thesis or dissertation and is based on the rigorous model of the scientific method used in theoretically oriented, academically directed research pursuits. For example, the common survey course in research methods found in graduate degree programs in these fields covers experimental and other methods for developing and testing hypotheses. The danger of this approach to research is that it tends to orient the HRD practitioner to the view that research is something associated with academic journals and, in its ultimate execution, tests the adequacy of theories and hypotheses. That is, research means experimental designs, theories, variables, statistical analysis, and testing hypotheses. The quality of the research depends on how well it complies with all the traditional canons of science. The kinds of questions that animate theoretically oriented research include the following: How strong was the research design? How well defined and developed was the hypothesis? Has the problem been studied before? Did the evidence support or refute the hypotheses being tested (Graziano & Raulin, 1993)?

There are two particularly important criteria that capture the essence of theoretically oriented scientific research. To the extent that a research project is weak on either criterion, the research and any conclusions derived from it are suspect. One criterion is validity, and the other is reliability. *Validity* refers to the degree of accuracy possible in the research (Kirk & Miller, 1986). A research procedure can make mistakes: Does a survey of employees about their managers' coaching practices really indicate how well the managers coach, or might it simply indicate the degree to which employees like or dislike their bosses, regardless of their coaching ability? How accurately does the survey answer questions about coaching style and effectiveness? Without confidence in the validity of the research, there can be little confidence in the conclusions. Validity can be divided into two distinct dimensions (Krathwohl, 1985).

1. *Internal validity.* The research should be designed so that the nature of the relationship between predictor and outcome variables (strong, weak, or nonexistent) can be clearly seen. A poorly designed research project means that there may be other, competing explanations for the data. These threats to validity[1] raise questions about the accuracy and value of the conclusions of the research. For example, to test whether allowing voluntary attendance at a training program increases trainee participation and motivation, a series of programs are offered at the downtown headquarters from 4 to 7 p.m. and, as might be expected, there are few takers. Does low attendance mean voluntary attendance is a failure or does it mean that any program offered at an inconvenient location after normal business hours will fail?

2. *External validity.* The conditions of the study should be as similar as possible to the conditions found in the real world. For example, a common complaint about much university-based laboratory research in industrial organization psychology is that it is done using 20-year-old undergraduates in very artificial conditions. To what extent can conclusions reached in such studies be applied to middle-aged mid-managers in midsize firms?

Reliability refers to the consistency of the measurement process over time. That is, different measures of the same phenomena should yield similar results. A research procedure can be reliable but not valid. Consider the management potential instrument on which I have been working, the CMPI (Clardy Management Potential Indicator). Although I am convinced of its originality and brilliance, to the uninitiated it would appear to be a simple measuring tape hung on a wall. To measure management potential, prospects stand against the wall, and I obtain a reading such as 64 or 72 (in inches). The higher the reading, the greater the person's potential. Although I can obtain consistent or reliable readings on successive administrations of the instrument to the same person, most women on whom the instrument has been field-tested protest that it is not an accurate or valid predictor of management potential. Research plans and procedures should be as valid and reliable as possible in their design and execution.

Concern about validity and reliability highlight the thorny problem of error in data collection and analysis: Errors in data collection will likely mean mistakes in the conclusions. The scientific research process is designed to set up guards and checkpoints to reduce the possibility of error in all phases of a research project.

In short, then, theoretically oriented scientific research is characterized by the following features:

- The research is driven to test hypotheses derived from theory.
- The research uses experimental or quasiexperimental research designs.

- Rigorous controls over the conduct of the research are applied to reduce threats to validity.
- A sample of subjects, preferably chosen at random to represent a larger population, is selected and studied in the research.
- The data are analyzed, often statistically, to compare differences in outcomes between control and treatment groups.
- Findings are put into a report for journal publication.

Applied HRD Research

For the typical HRD practitioner, this orientation lacks relevance for the research projects that person faces every day. Rather, the HRD practitioner is interested in answering such questions as:

- How big or severe is the problem in this organization?
- Where is the problem located?
- What will it take to correct it?
- Was the intervention used an effective solution to the problem?

The horizon of applied research is the specific problem found in a specific organization at a specific time, not the development of theories and models, as is the case for theoretically oriented research.

For HRD practitioners, the model of theoretically oriented research may seem alien and remote. Organizational decision makers who employ HRD practitioners tend to care about HRD research only to the extent that it is necessary for solving performance problems.[2] Correspondingly, little energy is consumed wondering whether some hypothesis will be supported by the data or whether the results will be published. Indeed, either for proprietary or public relations reasons, decision makers may insist that the findings be kept confidential.

Thus, applied HRD research is distinctive—it uses the methods and principles of science whenever possible, but it operates in different ways and for different purposes. First, the focus of applied research is on diagnosing and solving operating problems, not on discovering or testing hypotheses. Indeed, decision makers care less about methodological sophistication and more about timely, efficient solutions. There is often a bias toward action, toward using the information, and away from analysis for its own sake. Second, the value of applied research comes from how well problems are addressed, not from how much it contributes to theory. There are specific audiences, including but not limited to organizational decision makers, to whom HRD research has immediate interest. The value of the research depends on the extent to which those interests are adequately addressed.

Third, HRD research is intimately connected to the intervention used to address the problem. As discussed more fully in the following sections, there are three main points of contact between research and the HRD intervention: problem detection, solution planning, and intervention evaluation. Fourth, there is often no distinction between sample and population. There is often little interest in or chance to extend the findings of the research beyond the immediate group included in the research.

Fifth, unlike the "subjects" in theoretically oriented research, who have no vested interest in the outcome of the research, the personnel included in applied HRD projects are typically working adults with job security and career concerns. There are several implications to this. Applied-research participants, aware that the findings could have personal consequences, may seek to present themselves in the most favorable light. Distorted answers are a natural expectation. On the other hand, the degree of cooperation from participants may depend on whether their contributions will be confidential and protected. There may also be legal and ethical issues involved. Personnel actions based on research may be subject to judicial review, for example, if employees are adversely affected.

Sixth, applied HRD research must often be conducted without the kinds of rigorous controls deemed so important in scientific studies. At the job site, there may be a number of factors at play at the same time, making it very difficult to differentiate the true effects of a training program from the persistent background noise of exhortations, fear, organizational culture, technology, changes in markets, and general economic conditions.

The distinction raised between applied HRD research and theoretically oriented scientific research is not meant to suggest an adversarial relationship between the two, for the canons of the scientific method function as guidelines for how to collect, analyze, and interpret data in applied research projects. Some of the distinguishing characteristics of applied and theoretical research are shown in Table 1.1.[3]

There are two important points that applied HRD researchers should draw from this comparison. First, the research project should be well planned. The plan should include specific procedures for controlling data collection and analysis. Second, the research and the data collection process should be designed to be as valid and reliable as possible. Threats to validity should be anticipated and ways found to offset those threats.

TABLE 1.1 Comparison of Applied and Theoretical Research

	Theoretically Oriented Research	*Applied Research*
Main purpose	Hypothesis testing	Solving operating problems
Controls over intervention and data collection	Critical and should be included as part of research	Not always possible
Research subjects or participants	May not be personally affected by research	Research outcomes would often have personal impact
Group studied	Sample preferably drawn at random	Group is often the population
Intervention	Used as experimental treatment to test hypothesis	Used to solve problem
Assessment of quality of research based on	Validity and reliability	Utility of information obtained
Research conclusions targeted for	Publication in scientific, academic journal	Organizational decision makers

■ The Stages of HRD Research

There are three primary points at which applied research can serve the HRD process. The specific techniques employed at each point in the process use a common set of well-defined data collection procedures (discussed in Chapters 2 and 3). The three stages at which research is most critical for effective execution of HRD programming are shown in Figure 1.1.

The first stage uses research to identify the kinds of performance problems that HRD can and should address. Traditionally, this step has been called *training needs assessment*. Four specific research applications are presented here: an organizational assessment to identify problems, a performance problem analysis to isolate the causes of the problem (and determine whether training is the indicated solution), a trainee assessment to determine which employees need what kind of training, and a readiness for change review to judge whether the organization is ready to support the changes training should produce. These applications are detailed in Chapters 4 and 5.

Once a performance problem that can be addressed through a HRD program has been identified, the next major research opportunity is to prepare a solution

Front-End Assessment:
Identifying HRD Problems

PERFORMANCE PROBLEMS

Assessing Adequacy of
HRD Solution

Developing and
Implementing
HRD Solutions

Figure 1.1. The Three Stages of HRD Research

(that is, some kind of organized process for learning the abilities needed to perform current or future jobs). But what should a program include and how should it be designed to be maximally effective? Chapter 6 looks at several research-based ways to address this question. A competency profile isolates the specific skills that should be taught. Ascertaining certain learner characteristics, such as literacy skills or learner motivation, may be critical for appropriate program planning. Training materials unique to the program may need to be developed. Finally, drafted training programs should be pilot tested prior to full-scale implementation.

Chapter 7 looks at the last major stage of HRD research, program evaluation, of which there are two kinds. Formative evaluations occur while a program is in operation to determine what changes or improvements may be needed. Summative evaluations describe the effects of a completed program. Four different approaches to summative program evaluation are considered, including an experimental model, a goal-based model, a stakeholder-drive model, and an effects-based model. Guidelines for planning and conducting an evaluation are presented. Table 1.2 provides a road map of the different applications of HRD research presented in this book.

One message repeated in almost every management and business volume these days is the importance of sound HRM and development practices for

TABLE 1.2 Overview of HRD Research Methods Presented in This Book

Research Stage	Principal Areas of Research Focus	Special Applications
Identifying HRD problems: front-end assessment	Organizational assessment	• Performance indicators • Benchmarking • Business and human resources plans • HRD audit
	Performance problem analysis	
	Trainee assessment	• Job and task analysis • Ability assessment
	Readiness for change review	• Review checklist
Developing and implementing HRD solutions	Competency profile	
	Identify learner characteristics	• Literacy/math abilities • Motivation to learn
	Customize instructional materials	
	Program review and pilot testing	
Assessing solution adequacy	Formative evaluation	
	Summative evaluation	• Models: Experimental Goal-based Stakeholder-driven Effects-based

organizational survival and competitive advantage. Training is an essential ingredient. More than ever, training needs to be an effective and powerful contributor to the well-being of any organization, and effective applied HRD research is critical to this success.

■ **Notes**

1. Several years ago, I was asked to assess the administrative support system of a large bank. Under this system, all secretaries reported to a central administrator. In other words, no secretaries

reported directly to the manager for whom they worked. Few were surprised when a user satisfaction survey sent to managers was generally negative and indicated that there was a widespread interest in doing away with this system. However, the central administrator of the support system had difficulty accepting that conclusion. For her, the real explanation was that the data or the subsequent analyses were wrong. She recalculated all the original responses herself to prove that the analysis was wrong. (It wasn't.) The point of the story is that if research results are to be believed, it is essential to do everything possible to rule out competing alternative explanations for the results.

There are a number of threats to the validity of a research project (Campbell & Stanley, 1963; Cook & Campbell, 1979). For example, *history* means that some event other than the treatment produces the observed changes. Consider a situation in which a "rich" sales incentive program is started about the same time as a sales training program; company sales increase. What was the real cause of the increase—the training or the lucrative incentive plan? Another threat is *maturation,* when subjects change normally. One would expect the performance of new employees to improve after 6 months on the job, regardless of whether there was an employee orientation program. Other threats include the effects of

1. *Testing.* Assume a group of trainees are given a test of what they know about a topic both before and after a training program, and there was a noticeable average increase in test scores. Was the increase due to real learning or simply to the fact that they became "test smart" after taking the test the first time?

2. *Changes in measurement instruments.* What if you use a different test after the training is over, and there are still gains in average scores? Do the gains represent real learning, or was the second test easier to take?

3. *Selection or turnover effects.* Do changes in test scores reflect the fact that the people in the program were somehow different from the normal population (selected because they were "smarter" or "dumber") or that there was some loss of either smarter or dumber participants by the time the second test was taken?

To combat these potential threats to validity, experimental or quasiexperimental research designs are recommended. HRD practitioners should be aware of these designs to fully appreciate published research. In addition, some kinds of HRD program evaluations may use these models for evaluation purposes.

2. This is not to ignore the fact that many decision makers appreciate and support theoretically oriented research, regardless of whether there is a direct payoff or not to their organizations. Many a thesis or dissertation was made possible through the kindness of these management strangers. The point here is that the *primary* interest of *most* managers is how HRD research can be useful in addressing specific organizational problems, not in its potential value in refining theory.

3. These portraits are idealized views to highlight the differences between the two approaches. In practice, the differences are not so stark, especially in the case of field research, where research activities may serve dual masters of theory and application.

2

DATA COLLECTION

Planning, Tests, and Observation

■

Applied research in training and development involves collecting information to use in planning, developing, and evaluating HRD programs. This chapter and the next look at methods, tools, and techniques for collecting the information needed for any of those activities. Included here are reviews of how to design, develop, and implement methods for gathering information as part of a research project. These tools and techniques can serve any number of research applications. The data collection techniques presented here are the *how to* aspects of research; the research applications in the following chapters address *what kind* of information to collect. Interviews, for example, can be used in all phases of front-end assessment, program planning, and evaluation. Interviews are methods for collecting information; the kind of information that should be collected through an interview depends on the purpose of the research activity. Productive research results when the mechanics of how to collect information effectively are joined with a substantive focus on what kind of information to collect.

This chapter begins with a meditation on research mistakes by considering this question: What are some of the potential sources of error in data collection? Some basic steps for reducing the likelihood of making those errors during a research project are then offered. A general-purpose model for planning a project is then described. In Chapters 2 and 3, four methods for collecting data—tests, observations, surveys, and interviews—are examined. This chapter looks at the specific issues and procedures associated with testing and observation. The next chapter will review these same issues and procedures for survey questionnaire design and interviewing techniques. The intention of both chapters is to provide a quick, practical guide for developing and using valid and reliable techniques for collecting the information needed as part of any training and development research activity.

■ Data Collection: Pitfalls and Promises

The acid test of any HRD research project is that *usable* information is collected that helps in planning, developing, and evaluating a training and development program. Usable information is often easier described than produced, however. To be usable, the HRD practitioner must have confidence in the accuracy of the information collected. Yet there are a number of potential problems that may call into question the accuracy and usefulness of collected data. Identifying these sources of error is necessary to plan ways to avoid them.

Common Research Errors

The discussion of validity and reliability in Chapter 1 introduced the problem of error in data collection. Obviously, one competing explanation for any research conclusion is that the data behind the conclusion are wrong because the data collection process was flawed or biased. There are several common sources of error possible in any process of collecting information (Selltiz, Jahoda, Deutsch, & Cook, 1964):

1. *Random mistakes in recording information.* For example, a survey interviewer mistakenly circles a 2 (not agree) rather than the 3 (not sure) given by the person being interviewed.
2. *Sampling error.* The sample can be too small or the people in the sample may represent a biased group. For example, a training needs assessment sent to the poorest-performing 10% of 100 technicians would likely create a distorted image of the training needs of all 100 technicians.
3. *Subject misrepresentation or lying.* The people being interviewed or observed may not yield accurate information, especially if they feel the information may be used

against them. They may simply give incorrect responses or adjust their performance to be more acceptable.

4. *Investigator bias.* Researchers may look at a problem through the lens of their
specialty. Thus, an auditor might interpret a performance problem as resulting
from a lack of controls, whereas an organization development specialist might see
the same problem in terms of lack of trust or resistance to change.

5. *Faulty instrumentation.* The instrument used to collect the information may be
poorly constructed and have low validity or reliability.

Given this list of potential problems, the methods and procedures used to
collect information become particularly important and should be designed to
reduce, control, or eliminate as many sources of error as possible. This means
making the research process as valid and reliable as possible. The following
precautions can help reduce the likelihood of these errors infecting your data
collection activities, thereby increasing your confidence in the usefulness of the
data collected.

1. *Standardize the process.* This means making all aspects of the data collection
procedure as consistent and uniform as possible. Standardization is particularly
important for recording data. For example, a problem with unstructured interviews
is a lack of common questions: The same interviewer may ask different questions
across interviews or different interviewers may do the same. Either way, the result
can easily be a potpourri of information that is not comparable. Standardizing what
kinds of information to obtain and how that information will be recorded will help
produce useful data.

2. *Pretest the procedure.* Before using a procedure to collect data, try out the
procedure first to see if it works as intended. Pretest the procedure on people who
are similar to the ones to whom it will eventually be administered. Look at whether
you are collecting the information you want in the ways designed; if not, make
any necessary improvements.

3. *Train and practice.* If several people will be involved in collecting the data (say,
different interviewers), they should be trained in how to use the instrument. They
should practice using it and handling any problems. This group should be trained
until members are sufficiently consistent in recording information for your purposes. Part of this preparation should also include tips and techniques for reducing
respondent impulses for misrepresentation, including communicating confidentiality protections, reacting in a nonjudgmental, value-neutral way, allowing respondents a period of time to warm up to an observer before beginning the actual data
collection activities, and encouraging respondent commentary through active
listening and related methods of asking questions and eliciting opinions.

4. *Supervise and monitor data collection.* Plan on checking out data collectors,
especially during early stages. If you are undertaking primary data collection, plan
to incorporate as many of these safeguards as possible.

5. *Avoid investigator bias by keeping an open mind.* This is particularly important during the early, exploratory stages of research, when a researcher is simply trying to understand what is going on. Avoid trying to fit what the respondents are saying into preset categories such as auditing or organization development. Listen to how the people being interviewed or observed describe and explain what is going on.

6. *Obtain an adequate number of observations.* This means using a sampling plan that is representative of the full range of people or events under study. For large populations, a random selection procedure is best; competent texts in statistics discuss specific techniques of random selection and recommended sample sizes. For small populations, it may be possible to interview everyone. This rule applies not only to people but also to processes. For example, if you are studying the customer services behaviors in a retail chain, you should make sure you observe behaviors at a number of different stores at various times, day and night, throughout the week.

Planning the Research

All of these tactics for reducing error can be addressed and managed through a research plan. For any research project, the first step is to develop a plan for data collection and analysis. The research plan involves identifying what kind of information is needed, from whom, how it will be collected, and how the information will be analyzed and reported. A well-considered research plan is important because it forces the researcher to think through how the information will be collected and analyzed. This is critical because researchers should anticipate how they will process the information before they collect it. Plan for data collection and subsequent analysis at the same time.

An effective HRD research plan should include the following sections:

1. Background. What is the history and context of the HRD project being researched?

2. A statement of what information is needed and how that information will be used. Identify any relevant "stakeholders" in the research.

3. The population to which the results of the research will be applied. In applied research with small and midsize organizations, the population to be covered and the sample used may be the same.

4. The data collection process, including
   a. what the data collection procedures are (surveys, interviews, and so on) and any specific instrument(s); to be used (such as the Myers Briggs Type Inventory or a published test in Spanish, for example);
   b. the timing of data collection: when data will be collected; and
   c. if a sample of the population will be used, how that sample will be selected and what size it will be.

CHART 2.1 Example of a Research Plan

Management Readiness for Change Research Plan

1. **Background.** A management training program for the department managers of XYZ Corporation's Field Services Division is indicated. Prior to final approval, the commitment of the division's senior managers to the training must be assessed.

2. **Information needed.** Two kinds of information are needed: division manager awareness of the need for training and division manager willingness to support the training. This information will be compiled and reported to the general manager to advise whether there is sufficient support for training, whether any preliminary work needs to be done with the management group to build support for the training, or both.

3. **Population covered.** 10 senior managers of the Field Services Division.

4. **Data collection process.**
   a. Data collection procedure: Personal interview
   b. Instrumentation: Readiness for Change interview guide
   c. Timing of data collection: All interviews conducted during a 2-week period, prior to final planning decisions about the training
   d. Sampling: Since all 10 managers will be interviewed, not a factor

5. **Methods of analysis.** An analysis table will be used, listing each manager along the top row. The far-left column will list specific awareness and willingness issues raised in the interviews. Each cell will contain summaries of the comments made. A column on the far right will summarize all observations into a final assessment.

6. **Report format.** The report will include an executive summary, an opening section covering the importance of management support and the issues assessed, a section describing the research itself, a reproduction of the analysis table, and a final section on recommendations.

7. **Project plan.** The report should be completed before the end of August 19xx.
   a. Steps: (1) Send out letter requesting interview, (2) schedule interviews, (3) conduct interviews, and (4) prepare and present report.
   b. Budget: NA.

---

5. Methods of analysis. Identify how the data will be coded or classified, what statistical methods (if any) will be applied, and how the information will be summarized and compared. Preparing blank, formatted tables that show the kinds of analysis to be conducted can be very helpful (Miles & Huberman, 1984).

6. The format of the report, such as the table of contents or the sequence of topics to be covered.

7. Resources required, budget, and timetable. If the research requires approval, a project management plan that includes a list of resources, a budget, and some kind of timetable or Gantt chart can be useful. See Chart 2.1 for a format for a general research plan.

■ Tests

Tests are a fitting place to begin discussing data collection techniques for use with learning programs. A *test* is any structured, systematic set of stimuli to which the person's responses can be scored or placed on a scale indicating the extent to which the person possesses the factor or construct being measured (Kerlinger, 1973, p. 492). Although the stimulus in a test can be an inkblot or a set of drawings, in the context of training, *stimuli* usually refer to statements to which the respondent expresses some degree of agreement or preference or to questions that assess how much the respondent knows about some topic.

There are many tests available, including aptitude or intelligence tests, personality tests, and tests of values or attitudes. For research in training, one very important type of test is the achievement test, which indicates the person's degree of mastery or proficiency in some field of knowledge. Although some tests should be administered only by trained psychologists, others may be available for use by noncertified HRD practitioners. A variety of tests can be administered as part of management or organization development programs. In some cases, the tests help individual learners pinpoint their management style, such as tests measuring a person's position on the Managerial Grid (Blake & Mouton, 1978) or Least Preferred Coworker (Fiedler, Chemers, & Mahar, 1977). Other tests are available for diagnosing working conditions, team operations, and so forth.

An important issue in testing involves how test data will be evaluated. Two approaches are possible. In a *norm-referenced* approach, a person's test score is ranked against the scores of all other test takers. In this way, a test taker may be said to be within one standard deviation of the test average (the area around the average where two out of three test scores are found) or to be in the top quartile (top 25%) of scores. Such scores indicate how well the test taker did in comparison with others but may not provide a good indication of how much the person really knows. For example, it might be of little comfort to discover that your physician scored in the top 10% of his basic biology class if the average grade for the class was a 10 out of 100 possible points. A second approach is called *criterion-referenced*. Here, test performance is compared to an existing set of standards, not to how well other test-takers do (Sackett & Mullen, 1993). In this approach, it is possible for all trainees to pass or to fail, depending on the extent to which they successfully achieve specified learning outcomes. For training purposes, criterion-referenced testing is usually recommended for evaluating test scores, particularly in terms of learning outcomes.

Given the wealth of developed and validated tests that are commercially available, the HRD practitioner should usually look for published tests first.[1] Otherwise, there are a variety of procedures for constructing scaled tests with high validity and reliability (see, for example, Morris, Fitzgibbon, & Lindheim, 1987b). However, such procedures usually require specialized skills and protocols (Crocker & Algina, 1986), and in most cases the HRD practitioner should acquire professional assistance if a specialized test must be developed from scratch. If a test is used to decide personnel actions such as selection, promotion, training admission, or graduation, or is used for compensation decisions, such as part of a pay-for-skills plan, the HRD practitioner should be aware of potential legal issues associated with using the test. For these uses, the practitioner should be able to report the validity and reliability of the test as a defense against possible adverse impact problems.

There are certain considerations that should guide the practitioner in selecting a commercially available test for use as a data collection instrument:

1. *Find a test with sufficient validity and reliability.* Any number of "tests" make their way to the market; some are strong and others are not. A test's reputability will increase to the extent that the producer of the test has a report or validation study available that details the theoretical basis of the test, explains how the test was constructed, and provides evidence of test validity and reliability.

2. *Establish the job or training relevancy of the test.* The items covered by the test should bear some demonstrable linkage with the training or the job. Relevance can be assessed by a two-column chart that lists either training program content or job duties in the left column and test content in the right column. The test should adequately match the significant portions of the training or the job.

3. *Pick a test that can be administered openly and easily.* Tests that take a long time to complete or that are complicated to score are less attractive than those that cover most of the same topics more efficiently. Furthermore, in HRD, copies of tests can be obtained easily, then reproduced and used without approval. Not only do such practices violate copyright laws, but they may nullify the test's value because its results cannot be fully explained. In some cases, unlicensed testing may make the person giving the test personally liable should there be any adverse consequences from the test.

4. *Identify the passing score.* Particularly for criterion-referenced tests, it is important to set the level of the passing score fairly and accurately. One relatively simple approach is to administer the test to known groups of masters and novices. Masters may be identified by nomination from upper managers, coworkers, or staff personnel familiar with employee performance, or by review of performance records that indicate the top group. Analyze the results to determine the level of test performance that seems to mark off masters from all others. Set the cutoff score at the lowest score that would seem to include most of the masters (Panell

& Laabs, 1979; Shrock, Mansukham, Coscarelli, & Palmer, 1986). Another approach recommends that subject matter experts (SMEs) rate the probability (from 0 to 1) that a minimally competent person would answer each item on a test correctly. The cutoff score is the sum of the item proportions. Thus, on a 5-item test, SMEs agree on the following respective probabilities for correctly answering the five items: .2, .8, .5, .7, and .3, for a total of 2.5, which would become the minimum criterion score for passing the test (Maurer & Alexander, 1992).

Special Application: Learning Achievement Test

There is one type of test that an HRD practitioner should be able to develop: a learning achievement test for a program of instruction that assesses trainee understanding and comprehension of material covered by the instruction. Test questions have a correct answer that the test-taker answers either correctly or not. Such tests are a primary means for evaluating the learning that results from an HRD program. Other evaluation devices, such as behavioral rating scales, work samples, and interviews with or surveys of coworkers or customers, can also be used to directly or indirectly assess learning outcomes.

The procedures for developing a sound learning achievement test are relatively straightforward (Benson & Clark, 1982; Denova, 1979; Morris et al., 1987b). The work begins by identifying to whom the test will be given and planning the domain (or content area) that the test will cover. Within these parameters, actual test development can commence.

1. *Prepare a table of specifications to guide the development of test items.* A table of specifications lists the content areas covered by the training along the top row; down the left column is arrayed a learning hierarchy. The most widely known learning hierarchies were produced by Bloom and associates (1956; Krathwohl, Bloom, & Masia, 1964). For example, their cognitive learning hierarchy lists six different levels of learning performance a person can demonstrate with regard to a field of knowledge, beginning with reciting the knowledge (rote recall), then progressing through comprehension, application, analysis, synthesis, and evaluation. A table of specifications allows the test developer to plan the test by weighting content and types of test items.

   Table 2.1 shows an example of a table of specifications for a test on employment selection for supervisory trainees. Here, three content areas are noted: employment laws, interviewing techniques, and company policies and procedures. Three learning levels are stressed: comprehension, application, and analysis. The table shows the relative importance of each content domain and the kinds of learning that should be demonstrated in each domain.

2. *Develop a pool of items.* After specifying the type of test items needed, writing the test items begins. Plan on writing two times the number of items that will be

TABLE 2.1 Table of Specifications (in Percentages) for Learning Achievement,
Test for Employment Selection Training

	Employment Laws	Interviewing Techniques	Company Policies	Subtotal
Comprehension	25	10	10	50
Application	0	30	10	40
Analysis	15	0	0	10
Subtotal	40	40	20	100

a. Subtotals indicate the relative weight of importance assigned to either the content area or the type of proficiency expected in that content area.

needed. Select the item format to be used: true/ false, multiple choice, matching items, fill-in-the-blank, short-answer, or essay responses. There are certain guidelines to keep in mind when writing test items (Canter, 1987; Denova, 1979):

a. the items should be clearly written, using terms that are familiar to the test-taker,

b. the nature of the desired response must be clearly stated (consider: "Product X's best feature is that it is: *a great product,*" where the type of desired response is ambiguous, vs. "Compared to our competition, the pricing feature for Product X is: *lowest on the market,*" where the type of desired response is indicated),

c. avoid making the lead-in phrase (or *stem*) too complicated or too qualified,

d. avoid *all/none of the above* responses or universal qualifiers (such as *always* or *never*),

e. in multiple-choice formats, keep all responses plausible and approximately the same length,

f. randomly place correct responses (e.g., so that all the correct multiple choice answers are not *d*).

Edit the items and prepare a working draft of the test, formatted into a test booklet. For example, the cover page to the test should state the purpose of the test and refer to the learning objectives it covers. Instructions for completing the test (such as a time limit) or using aids (such as calculators), or examples of how to answer certain questions, should also be readied (Rosenberg & Smitley, 1983), along with a separate answer sheet, if needed.

3. *Validate the content.* Have SMEs—personnel widely regarded as very knowledgeable about the procedure, product, or subject area based on their education, training, or job experience—review the test. Minimally, the experts should agree on the answers. In addition, give them a copy of the table of specifications: They should agree on which test items belong to which cells in the table. If there is disagreement, rework the item or drop it.

Administer the test to a sample of respondents. Analyze item responses in terms of item discrimination, and keep the most discriminating items. For example, on a multiple-choice test, assume that all respondents answered c to a question 8, with c as the correct response. For question 9, responses were equally spread across answers a through d. Question 8 does not discriminate among respondents, whereas question 9 does. Items such as 9 should be kept and items such as 8 should be dropped. More sophisticated studies of reliability (split half, parallel forms, or test-retest) may also be conducted and the results statistically analyzed.

■ Direct Observation

Direct observation is just that: placing oneself in a setting or situation to watch and record events as they occur. The classic example of direct observation in research occurred at the Western Electric Hawthorne Works, when investigators observed work teams as they went about their duties of wiring switchboards and the like (Roethlisberger & Dickson, 1950). More recent applications of direct observation involved studying work methods and time and motion studies (Drury, 1990).

Like the interviewing tactics discussed in Chapter 3, observational techniques can be either unstructured or structured. Unstructured observation occurs when the researcher enters the situation without any preset categories or observation checklist. Such an approach is well suited for exploratory research aimed at familiarizing the researcher with a new situation. A structured observation process is one that is systematic, focused, and controlled by some kind of observation schedule. For example, Bales (1951) created a highly structured set of categories of behavior in a group, which in turn is used for observing and classifying group interactions.

Direct observation may be particularly useful to double check events reported by trainees and others in surveys or interviews. That is, rather than relying exclusively on trainees' or managers' reports about changes in job performance, the HRD practitioner can make direct, on-site observations of how managers hold meetings, how service representatives work with clients, or whether trained behaviors are being used on the job, to collect additional data.[2]

The advantages of direct observation as a method of collecting data are immediacy and depth. One can inspect the entire situation and notice factors and circumstances that might otherwise go unreported, yielding a richness in perception and awareness often missing from surveys and interviews. There are disadvantages to direct observation, though. First, the presence of an observer, no matter how passive, can create *experimenter effects* in which the people being observed act differently than normal. Second, depending on the approach used, there may be a lack of standardized data, which can create problems in coding and analysis. Third, direct observation is both time-consuming and limited in scale. To be thorough, one must be willing to observe multiple instances of the process being observed over a period of time. Furthermore, there is a "line of sight" problem: One can observe only that which is visible. Thinking processes or behind-the-scenes work may be missed.

Nonetheless, direct observation can yield rich data describing the setting and conditions of the unit of study. Direct observation can also be used to record people's communications in the situation. There are three kinds of data that are most easily produced from direct observation: detailed descriptions of physical settings and social arrangements, interactions, and processes; direct quotations or records of what was said; and documentation of signs, posters, announcements, and other visual and auditory materials present (Patton, 1980). Effective direct observation includes the following procedures (Boice, 1983; Brandt, 1981; Peak, 1965).

1. *Record events as they unfold, without censoring or judging them.* Describe what happens as fully and faithfully as possible. Use direct quotes whenever possible. If you cannot make notes while watching events, make notes about things as soon as possible thereafter.

2. *Take complete notes.* Describe the setting and context fully: What was the situation, who was present, what did they do, and when? Keep three kinds of logs during data collection: first, an observation log that contains what is observed; second, a commentary log of questions, issues, problems, and interpretations that occur to you while observing or interpreting; and third, a log of methodological notes that tracks what you did, any research method problems, procedures followed, and so forth.

3. *Be attentive to possible sources of misinformation.* Expect your initial presence to make people uneasy and to distort their reactions. Plan to use these early observations as both a practice period for you and a get-acquainted period for the people being observed. Not including this information as part of the subsequent analysis may be a good idea.

4. *Look for the ordinary and typical.* It is easy to be drawn to the exotic or unusual.

5. *Use checklists or rating scales whenever possible.* Train observers in what to look for and how to use the checklist or schedule. Use more than one observer if possible.

Checklists or ratings scales can be particularly useful in observation. A checklist is a set of mutually exclusive categories of actions, behaviors, or conditions that may or may not be present. The observer simply notes whether the item is present or not. In addition, checklists or worksheets can be adapted to record other aspects of observed performance, such as the sequence of activities (by numbering the order in which activities occurred); the duration or length of activities (by noting starting and ending times); and spatial positioning or movement (by tracing the location or flow of people or objects across a floor plan).

With this information in hand, several kinds of summaries and analyses are possible. For example, a frequency count shows the total number of times an activity occurred. For example, meeting management skills could be assessed by observing the kinds of comments made during meetings. In a meeting run by one manager, for example, hostile remarks outnumbered tension-reduction remarks by almost two to one. Another kind of summary would be the percent of time spent on each task. Again, for the manager under study, hostile and defensive conversations consumed almost 50% of total meeting time. Finally, flow charts map areas of high and low traffic (Drury, 1990). In this meeting, two subgroups tended to sit together—but each group sat opposite the other.

The use of checklists is well illustrated in a study of nursing home quality of care (Shore, Lerman, Smith, Iwata, & DeLeon, 1995). In this case, a simple checklist format of over 20 distinct conditions was developed. The conditions were grouped into four categories: environment (e.g., safety and cleanliness), resident conditions (such as being groomed or free from injury), resident activity, and staff activity. Each item was defined with specific instructions for grading the presence (+) or absence (–) of that condition. For example, for the Supervision item in the Environment set, the instructions stated, "Score (+) if at least one staff member is present. Score (–) otherwise." Two researchers entered an area of the nursing home at the same time; the use of dual observers permitted an assessment of interobserver reliability. The observers followed a semirandom schedule in visiting the different areas of the nursing home, and no more than two rounds of observations were taken in each area on any given day. The observers completed the checklist about the conditions in the area at the time they were there. Frequency counts of the presence of each item were calculated by dividing the number of observed occurrences for any item (+) by the total number of possible observations for that item. Supervisors, for example, were present on the average for all areas observed 89% of the time.

Unlike checklists, which simply report on the binary presence or absence of some condition, rating scales measure the degree to which some condition is present by assigning a value based on observation. For example, to what extent do managers run well-organized meetings or to what degree do front-line employees demonstrate proper customer contact skills? All rating scales share certain characteristics (see Guilford, 1954). Some trait or phenomenon (such as meeting management behavior) is the focus. The trait or phenomenon may in turn be broken down into elements, such as clearly stating the purpose of the meeting, encouraging participation, and so forth. Grades or levels of possible performance are indicated. The grades are arrayed in some kind of progressive order, say, from least to most. One of the grades is selected as best representing the typical level of performance observed. A numerical value can be attached to each gradient that parallels the progressive ordering of the grades (e.g., 1, 2, 3, etc.).

Beyond this set of core features, rating scales may take various forms (DeVellis, 1991; Guilford, 1954). Numerical scales are sets of numbers with simple definitions (1 = not at all, 2 = to a limited degree, etc.). Each number is a discrete rating. Graphic rating scales add a continuous line to the numbers, so that a rating of 1.75 or 4.3 may be made. Behavior observation scales (BOS) apply frequency ratings to a comprehensive list of behaviors. For example, to what extent (1 = never, 2 = rarely, 3 = sometimes, 4 = usually, 5 = always) do customer service personnel use the customer's name at least once in a transaction? Behaviorally anchored rating scales (BARS) are detailed statements of behaviors for most or all the levels of the scale. Thus, on a 7-point scale, each point would be defined (or anchored) by a rich description of behaviors that characterize that behavior (Beatty & Schneier, 1977; Smith & Kendall, 1963). Mixed standard scales use a comprehensive set of behavioral statements. Three statements, representing superior, expected, and inadequate performance on a common performance dimension, are grouped together. The person being rated is judged on each statement, using one of three rating levels: better than, equal to, or worse than. Rosinger and associates (1982) developed a mixed standards scale with 78 job performances grouped into 26 sets for use in rating state troopers. The "stopping vehicles" set illustrates the scale. For this performance dimension, three job performances were identified: stopping vehicles for a variety of violations, stopping violators for speeding but considering other violations, and stopping only for speeding.

In general, a rating scale should be based on a job analysis that identifies key dimensions of performance (such as customer service, productivity, or inventory control). This step usually requires that a group of job incumbents, supervisors, or SMEs be asked for input. Once the broad dimensions of performance are identified and defined, specific behaviors for each dimension are identified. Then, different levels of actual performance for each behavior are described. Again, a group of job incumbents and supervisors should be used to create this list of performance levels. A group of personnel can be used to sort these performance levels to match the rating scale. Keep those performance level identifiers on which there is widespread agreement about placement, such as if three out of four personnel agreed that a statement indicates a 3 level on the scale.

Campbell and associates (1973) followed a similar procedure when developing a rating scale for department managers of a large chain of retail stores. They had a group of 20 store managers write five examples of effective and five examples of ineffective department manager behaviors. The researchers then grouped those statements into what became nine key dimensions of performance, including supervision of sales personnel, handling customer complaints, ordering merchandise, planning sales promotions, and assessing sales trends. In a second meeting, the group of 20 managers wrote examples of levels of performance for each performance dimension (using a 9-point scale). This larger list of performance levels was then sorted and placed at some point on the 9-point scale. Those items on which there was at least 75% agreement about placement were kept to define the level of performance on the rating scale. As a result of this process, there were nine separate rating scales keyed to critical areas of job performance. For each scale, there were nine progressive levels of behaviors characterizing each point on the scale.

There are several guidelines to remember in developing rating scales. First, don't use more gradients than there can be discriminations. Although there is no absolute rule, five to seven gradient levels can be used as a general guideline (DeVellis, 1991). Second, make sure the traits or phenomena being rated are clearly and specifically defined. Third, each rating scale should rate only one trait or aspect of a phenomenon. For example, there are a number of distinctive behaviors that can be found in running meetings (such as setting direction, monitoring progress, including everyone, etc.). There should be a separate scale for each behavior. Fourth, use clear definitions to identify each gradient ("Keeping group discussion focused on the stated topic"). The definitions should be behavioral and unambiguous. Fifth, the levels should be arrayed in a clear progressive fashion to represent a real scale; use SMEs to verify the rank ordering and pretest the instrument before it is used.

Regardless of the specific data collection device used, direct observation of people at work on the job can be threatening. Especially important is that the observation process be as nonthreatening as possible, and there are several recommended tactics for reducing the threat (Zemke & Kramlinger, 1982). First, undercommunicate far in advance. The people being observed should be notified about any upcoming observations with a low-profile, "not-much-to-it" memo well in advance of the actual visit. Second, when observing, be "boring, thick, and uninteresting" (p. 81). You want the people being observed to forget you are there; your job is to record, not make a big impression. Third, ask simple questions in a low-key manner. Fourth, keep the recording process as unobtrusive and discrete as possible.

Special Application: Work Samples
and Assessment Centers

A special kind of observation procedure is the assessment center or its sibling, work samples.[3] Although primarily used in the area of employee selection, the underlying process can also be used as part of applied HRD research, especially in the area of training needs identification and learning evaluation. The essence of either procedure is to create simulated situations that are miniature versions of everyday job tasks. For example, a work sample designed for selecting auto mechanics involved rigging a car with four different problems; an intake sheet listed the symptoms of car problems reported by the driver. The mechanic applicants were observed as they diagnosed and repaired the problems (Muchinsky, 1975). Assessment centers are larger versions of work samples, often using 5 or 10 different simulated situations (Thornton & Byham, 1982). Both procedures differ from tests in two ways: Scores are assigned based on rater observations (not on the respondent's answers to test items), and the procedures tend to assess demonstrated actions and behaviors (rather than cognitive processes).

Both procedures follow a common development path (Keil, 1981; Seegers, 1989).

1. Identify job duties. From that list, pinpoint which specific tasks (such as engine diagnosis) or dimensions of performance (such as planning, coaching, etc.) are to be assessed. The tasks or dimensions should be important to overall job performance.
2. Select and develop an exercise that is representative of the job. Use SMEs to help in both developing and critiquing the exercise.
3. Prepare the observation and rating procedure. A checklist or behaviorally anchored rating scale is preferable. Pretest this procedure for accuracy.
4. Train those who will do the rating.

■ Summary

Applied research in HRD means collecting information that can be used in planning, developing, or evaluating an HRD program. To be useful, the information must be credible. Unfortunately, the data collection process can create errors and mistakes. These potential problems can be offset by making the data collection process standardized and well managed. All these procedures can be anticipated in a research plan, a model for which has been presented.

Two types of data collection techniques discussed in this chapter were tests and direct observation of performance. For many purposes, the HRD practitioner should first look for commercially available tests with strong validity and reliability. However, the HRD practitioner should be capable of developing a learning achievement test when needed. To create an achievement test, a table of specifications can be particularly helpful. Direct observation is a valuable way to cross-check verbal and survey reports. Although direct observation may arouse concern in those being watched, there are ways to reduce that anxiety. Furthermore, to make sure the data being collected are as helpful as possible, the HRD practitioner is advised to develop and use checklists or rating scales as part of the observation process. These devices are also important as part of assessment centers or work sample activities.

■ Notes

1. One general-purpose source for locating tests is the volume by Sweetland and Keyser (1991). See also Morris, Fitzgibbon, and Lindheim (1987a), Chapter 4, and Morris et al. (1987b), Chapter 2, for information about other sources of test information.

2. The use of different kinds of research methods and data collection activities is a good way to strengthen the validity of a research project. If different research methods turn up evidence that points to the same results, more confidence can be put in the conclusion about those results. For example, it is one thing for sales trainees to score well on a test of their knowledge of certain sales techniques after a sales training program, and another for the researcher to conclude from the scores that the training was a success. If direct observation of trainee sales calls also indicates that they are using the techniques taught, then that conclusion is made stronger. In Chapter 7, this principle is called *triangulation*. See also the presentation by Brewer and Hunter (1989) on the value and tactics of multimethod research.

3. Downs (1985) proposed a further variation on this approach, "trainability" testing. Such a procedure would be useful when training is a critical milestone for future job success and other selection devices have not been useful. She offers shoe repairs as an example: Applicants are given basic instruction in how to reheel a shoe, then put through trials in which their performance is observed and scored. This procedure assesses how well trainees remember and carry out instructions.

3

DATA COLLECTION

Surveys, Interviews, Analyzing the Data, and Reporting Results

■

This chapter completes the review of data collection techniques by looking at the principles of survey questionnaire design and interviewing methods. As in the previous chapter, several special applications of each technique are also covered here. The Delphi method, for example, is a special type of survey questionnaire procedure. Likewise, focus groups and nominal group techniques are presented as special variants of interviewing methods. All the methods reviewed in this chapter are based on obtaining data in the form of direct reports, either verbal or written, from the persons contacted. These reports become the data used in analysis, planning, and preparation. Finally, the concluding section of this chapter presents some general guidelines for analyzing and reporting the results from the data collected.

■ Survey Questionnaires

A *survey questionnaire* is a written set of questions or items designed to solicit specific information from respondents using a standardized format. Unlike tests, though, there are no right or wrong answers to the questions. Furthermore, survey questionnaires are typically distributed and collected through the mail (postal or interoffice). With the advent of computer area networks, surveys can also be distributed through e-mail. Sproul (1986) found that e-mail responses tended to be quicker and had higher response rates; however, respondents tended to answer more at the scale extremes, especially on opinion items. Survey questionnaires may also be administered in person using survey interview procedures. (Rules for developing the survey questionnaire instrument will be reviewed in this section, and the methods of survey interviewing will be presented in the next section.) The results of the survey are presented as quantitative summaries of the sample being studied. In HRD, one common example of survey questionnaires is the employee opinion survey. A variation of the standard survey questionnaire is the Delphi method (described more fully on the following pages).

A survey questionnaire is a valuable method of collecting information when there is a large or dispersed population that needs to be reached at about the same time. Surveys allow information to be gathered quickly. By forcing answers into preset categories, the potential biasing effects of an interviewer are largely neutralized, and it is easy to tabulate and compare responses. However, although survey questionnaires may describe what a population is thinking, they are less able to explain why that population thinks as it does. That is, a survey may reveal the degree to which employees find training satisfactory but provide only a limited explanation for that finding.

The design of a survey questionnaire involves two main steps–preparing the cover letter and designing the survey questionnaire itself. Pretesting the survey questionnaire should be part of the design process.

The *cover letter* provides the opportunity to introduce the researcher and the research project, while arousing the participant's interest in completing and returning the survey. Print the cover letter on quality paper that includes the letterhead of the president or other executive official sponsoring the research. Indicate who is doing the survey and why it is being done. Offer a compelling reason for participating in the survey, such as emphasizing how helpful the information will be in improving working conditions. If a sample of respondents was picked from a larger population, describe how respondents were selected. State any conditions about confidentiality. In some cases, you can encourage returns by creating an incentive in which all respondents who fill out the survey and return it by a given date will have their names entered into a drawing for a prize or will receive a summary copy of the survey results.

An effective survey will help you answer all the questions for which you need information. Write the items at the reading level of the respondents, and use familiar terms and phrasing. Give the survey a meaningful and descriptive title. Make sure that the instructions for completing it (including the due date and how to return it) are clearly displayed. End the survey with a "thank you." If anonymity or confidentiality is being guaranteed, include that information in the introduction.

A survey questionnaire that is too simple or has an unclear purpose may deter people from finishing it. A survey that is too long may have a similar effect. Providing clear instructions and blocking the items into groups or sections can help avoid such problems.

Guidelines for writing the survey items include the following (Fowler, 1984; Fowler & Mangione, 1990; Williams, 1972).

1. Start with factual, nonthreatening questions first (dates, locations, times). The best procedure is to begin with items that require selecting from a set of answers, rather than beginning with open-ended questions. Compare "How much training did you receive for your current position? _____ none _____ minimal _____ satisfactory _____ more than needed" to "Describe the amount and type of training you received for this position."

2. Precede questions with any necessary instructions, such as, "There are four statements below. Please read all four before you respond." In some cases, the respondent may need to be prompted to recall a situation: "Think of the last time you had to confront another employee about a performance problem." Also, be careful when asking people to generalize about their own behaviors: Clearly state whether you are asking about what the person *usually* does or what she or he did *last time*.

3. Avoid wording that may encourage the person to distort or lie. Compare "Did you finish high school?" to "What was the last year of schooling you completed?"

4. For closed-ended questions, in which the respondent must select from a set of provided answers, make sure all possible answers are included or provide a default category. Look at what's wrong in this example: "How long have you been in your current job: Less than 1 year, 1-3, 4-6?" There are two problems: There is no category for people who have been employed 7 or more years or for those people who are not working.

5. Ask one question at a time. Consider this question: "What were the five best books you read last year?" There are really three distinct questions here: Did you read any books last year? Did you read more than five books? Of those, which were the best five?

6. Do not use unknown concepts. If you must, be certain to define the concept. This is important when using frequency rating terms such as *often* or *seldom*: "*Often* means about two out of every three times."

7. If you need biographical, identifying information (e.g., age, length of employment, job title, or department) to make comparisons among respondents, put those items

at the end of the survey. Restate confidentiality protections and indicate that the information will be used only for analysis and comparison purposes.

8. If certain information is critical, you may wish to verify answers by asking similar questions at two different points in the survey. Similar answers build faith in the accuracy of the answers. For example, assume you are surveying the incidence of drug use on the job. An early question might be, "How often have you seen illegal drugs used on the job?" Toward the end of the survey, you might ask, "I have seen illegal drug use on the job: never, once, two to three times," and so forth.

9. Pretest the questions and the procedure on a small sample of respondents. After presenting the people with the survey form to complete, ask them what problems they had in understanding instructions, following the flow or logic of the items, recording their answers, and so forth. Other red flags to watch for in the pretest include:

   a. lack of responses to open-ended questions that may indicate problems with wording or placement,

   b. lack of variance in responses to an item or a large number of "don't know" responses that may indicate a need for rewording, and

   c. a scaled item that is answered twice or has a written-in response that may indicate a need for rewording.

The layout and formatting of the questionnaire is important. The survey form should be clean and crisp, professionally designed and presented. The survey should be organized for easy use and displayed for convenient reference. Grouping sets of related items together into boxes or sections can help the flow. Instructions may be put in **bold** or UPPERCASE letters. Provide examples of how to answer any unusual formats. Use arrows or other marks to guide movement through the survey. In addition, make sure that the responses can be easily seen for coding or data input.

Special Application: Delphi Method

The Delphi method is a special variant of the survey questionnaire (Delbecq, Van de Ven, & Gustafson, 1975). Like the questionnaire, it uses a standard set of questions for gathering information. However, rather than the questionnaire being administered once to an ad hoc sample, a panel of individuals is chosen to participate on an ongoing basis in two or more rounds of surveys.

The Delphi method can be a good technique to use when you need to know or develop a consensus on options or issues relating to a proposed course of action or understand the range of opinions or assumptions on a current subject of interest. For example, assume you have a large number of geographically dispersed managers or employees from a number of different departments. You might want to know what they think are important training needs and also have them narrow that broad list into a smaller list of priority items. A Delphi-type survey would be appropriate. For example, a group of New Jersey public-sector executives went through three rounds of a Delphi study to identify training needs for a leadership development program (Olshfski & Joseph, 1991).

People are typically asked to participate on the panel because of their involvement in the subject or because of their special background in relation to the issue being investigated. Those affected by the program or experts on the subject are clearly important to include. Thus, an early step is to identify the qualifications that respondents should have to participate. There are no restrictions on the minimum number of respondents, although the more people involved, the richer the data and analysis.

The initial survey form should include a cover letter that explains the entire survey cycle and the intention of the study. The initial survey form is similar to a written brainstorming exercise and is intended to produce a large list of ideas and reactions about a general issue (such as barriers to action, perceived problems, or future developments). Therefore, the first form should include a few broad, open-ended questions (pretested) with plenty of room for written answers. After the initial survey is distributed and collected, a simple list of all responses, edited and grouped into categories, is compiled. A second survey form is prepared for distribution back to the panel, including the list of responses and containing new questions asking for clarification or commentary on those responses. In addition, panel members are asked to vote on the items in terms of their importance. For example, if there were 15 items, respondents could be asked to rank the items from 1 to 15; or if there were 40 items, they could be grouped into top-, moderate- and low-priority categories, then ranked within each category. The responses from round two can be summarized as shown in Table 3.1.

In the third (and typically last) round, panel members are sent the summary and asked for any final comments. This cycle of questions-responses-summary-feedback-questions may continue until a consensus is formed or sufficient information is obtained. The data from the final round should be reported and a copy sent to panel participants.

The Delphi method does require significant administrative time spent locating and obtaining the participation of panel members. There will be some decline in responses across the various rounds, so some follow-up effort should be planned to remind and encourage participants to respond. Furthermore, the data provided will be only as good as the expertise or judgment of the respondents. You can partially account for this factor by having respondents rate their own

TABLE 3.1 Summary of Delphi Survey Results

Item Number	Number of People Voting for This Item	Individual Rankings Given to This Item	Total Score
1	7	10, 9, 10, 9, 6, 10, 9	63
2	3	7, 4, 5	16
3	6	8, 6, 8, 5, 8, 6	41
4	6	5, 4, 6, 6, 7, 3	31

expertise on the topic. But again, the real intention of a Delphi procedure is to develop a consensus among participants, with precision being of secondary concern (Linstone, 1978). The Delphi survey takes time and requires panel members to be able to express themselves in writing.

■ Interviewing

An interview is a conversation or discussion focused on eliciting specific information from people about a topic of research interest (Kerlinger, 1973). Interviews are one of the primary methods of obtaining information and can occur in three different ways. First, the *unstructured* open interview is a free-ranging discussion without preset questions. This is best for open-ended exploration of a research topic, because it allows the person being interviewed to talk about the topic in whatever way that person wants. Unstructured interviews are natural partners to observation research methods (reviewed in Chapter 2). The problem with unstructured interviews is one of comparability: After multiple interviews, one may have a lot of information that is hard to integrate and compare.

Second, there is the *semi-structured* interview. Here, the interviewer has a set of prepared, general questions to guide discussion. However, the interviewer has the flexibility to probe, to ask questions in different sequences, and so forth. A potential problem with both of these interview formats concerns reliability due to interviewer error; that is, the more the variability between the interviews caused by differences in interviewer practices, the more potential for error.

Third, there is the *standardized* survey interview. In this form, the questions are precisely written and the conduct of the interviewer is tightly controlled so that the questions are read as worded in the order provided. The interviewer has very little freedom to vary from the format provided. As a result, a standardized survey interview becomes a personalized version of a survey questionnaire and should be used to obtain specific information on a set of preset categories from a large sample.

Interviews can yield information about people's experiences and behaviors, opinions, values and preferences, perceptions and feelings, recollection of events, knowledge, and biographical background. The ability of interviews to provide more thorough information about how people recall and consider events comes at a cost, however; it takes more time to gather data from interviews than from surveys. The trade-off is between the breadth of coverage in surveys and the depth of coverage in interviews. Standardized survey interviews occupy a middle position between the two.

Effective Interviewing Procedures

To some extent, there are certain universal skills required of all interviewers. These skills include the ability to establish a rapport with the persons being interviewed, to ask questions effectively, and to record information fully and faithfully. However, there are also differences in interviewing skills, depending on the type of interview being conducted. For example, unstructured and semistructured interviews often require the skills associated with therapeutic clinical interviews, including general, nondirective questioning; nonevaluative, active listening skills; and skillful probing (Egan, 1982).

Standardized interviewing requires additional skills. Standardization means that each person is asked the same set of questions in the same way. The foundation for effective standardized interviewing is the interview guide (the preparation of which was covered in the section on survey questionnaires). Guidelines for survey interviewing include the following:

1. Read the questions exactly as worded. Write down answers exactly as they are given.
2. Make it easy for the person to respond by using simple and direct questions.
3. When it is necessary to probe for information, do so in a nondirective yet consistent manner. For example, if the person being interviewed does not respond, reread the question. If the response is hazy or incomplete, use a standard probe, such as: "Tell me more about what you mean." If certain terms are unclear to the respondent, be ready to provide a definition.
4. If the respondent offers an answer that does not fit the coding scheme provided, the interviewer should teach the respondent how to answer correctly by saying that the answer must match one of the provided categories. Then the interviewer

should reread all options. The interviewer should not interpret the answer for the subject but rather insist that the subject select an appropriate response.

5. Train the interviewers to be neutral and nonjudgmental, that is, not to react with approval or disapproval to answers. Also, train the interviewer to establish a "climate" that is comfortable but motivated, professional and discreet. In general, the interviewer should be trained how to
   a. establish a relationship that will elicit cooperation,
   b. follow the interview guide, including the use of prompts or probes,
   c. handle questions or problems that may arise, and
   d. record the answers fully and completely.

6. Teach the subject how to be a good respondent by stating the purpose of the interview, identifying what the interview will cover, and explaining why it is necessary to carry out the interview in a standard manner.

7. Create a means for assessing the quality of the interviews such as listening to tape recordings of or observing some early interviews.

Special Application: Critical Incident Technique

One specific research technique with particular relevance to HRD combines surveys and interviews into a *critical incident technique* (CIT). The CIT was developed during World War II by Flanagan (1954) to aid in pilot assessment and training. He asked pilots, crewmen, supervisors, and other observers to describe either satisfactory or unsatisfactory examples of performing a task, such as flying a bomber. A *critical incident,* such as dealing with a navigational problem, was any relatively complete human activity that produced reasonably clear effects on the accomplishment of a mission, function, or task.

Several studies show how CIT can be used in HRD research. One study is again drawn from a military context: the evaluation of naval officer training curriculum (Glickman & Vallance, 1958). Incumbent officers on destroyers were asked to identify the situations that new ensigns might typically encounter and should be expected to handle when assigned to a ship for the first time. Over 1,000 critical incidents were identified and then sorted into groups. The knowledge and skills required in each incident were inferred. Incidents were classified as either taught or untaught in the training; in this case, about two thirds of the incidents were taught by the training at some point. For further analysis, the incidents were put on a second survey questionnaire that asked the commanding and executive officers of destroyers to identify how soon after coming on board a new officer should be expected to handle each situation well.

Another study, this time of front-line service employees in the hospitality and airline industries, sought to identify what those employees saw as "critical

EXHIBIT 3.1 Critical Service Incident Interview Guide

Put yourself in the shoes of customers of your firm. In other words, try to see your firm through your customer's eyes. Think of a recent time when a customer of your firm had a particularly satisfying (dissatisfying) interaction with you or a fellow employee. Describe the situation and exactly what happened.

1. When did the incident happen?
2. What specific circumstances led up to this situation?
3. Exactly what did you or your fellow employee say or do?
4. What resulted that made you feel the interaction was satisfying (dissatisfying) from the customer's point of view?
5. What should you or your fellow employee have said or done? (for dissatisfying incident only)

SOURCE: Reprinted with permission from *Journal of Marketing,* published by the American Marketing Association, Bitner, Booms, and Mohr, 1994.

service encounters" (Bitner, Booms, & Mohr, 1994). Employees from a variety of firms in these industries were interviewed and asked to describe any specific events, both good and bad, that affected customer satisfaction with the service they received. The basic interview guide used is shown in Exhibit 3.1.

Over 750 incidents were collected, almost 400 of which were examples of satisfactory performance. The incidents were classified into three major groups of actions: employee responses to service failures, responses to customer needs and requests, and unprompted, unsolicited actions.

CIT is a data collection procedure with great advantage for HRD, because it can be used to support virtually any aspect of HRD planning, from front-end assessment and competency profiling to curriculum design and evaluation. CIT is not without its drawbacks, however (Woolsey, 1986). First, the process requires time to administer and to analyze results. Second, CIT will not automatically identify the valid behaviors of successful job performance. The information collected includes respondent perceptions of what was done well or poorly.

The steps involved in conducting a CIT study are as follows.

1. Identify the domain of focus, such as "customer satisfaction" or "team leadership," from which activities are to be identified. The domain can be general, but it should be defined.
2. Specify the group whose on-the-job performance is to be studied (pilots, existing naval officers, front-line service representatives, etc.) and the personnel who will be asked to provide the information. These two groups may or may not be the

same. The respondents should be qualified (that is, have experienced or witnessed the processes in question).

3. Develop the data collection instrument and the data collection procedures. Since data may be collected through either a written survey, interview, or some combination of the two, the instrument should be formatted for the method used. As demonstrated in Exhibit 3.1, the actual instrument can be relatively short. The questions should ask about observed behaviors, not about psychological motives imputed to the performers.

   The instructions for completing the assessment should be clear. The instructions should include a definition of a *critical incident,* such as behaviors that are definitely effective or efficient (or ineffective/inefficient) in producing customer satisfaction (or whatever the domain may be) (Flanagan, 1954). In general, the instructions should prompt the respondent to recall specific incidents, both good and bad. Respondents should then be led through a series of questions designed to elicit details about the situation (who was present, where, when), the actions performed, and the effects of those actions (for example, the reactions of the customer). The instrument should be pretested for clarity and accuracy.

4. Administer the instrument to collect the data. Although surveys may be used exclusively, some interviewing is recommended so that sufficient detail will be produced. To this end, group interviews may be used. Andersson and Nilsson (1964) collected critical incidents about the behaviors of store managers in a Swedish grocery store chain. Data on the incidents were collected through questionnaires or individual interviews. Although interviews produced more incidents, both methods proved effective in generating critical incidents for use in determining training requirements of the store managers.

5. Analyze the data. Traditionally, each incident is written on a card, then intuitively sorted into groupings or categories. This may take several rounds. By using several raters, the degree of eventual agreement in sorting incidents can be assessed for interrater reliability. If two or more raters put a large percent (say, 85% or more) of the same incidents into the same groups, you may be highly confident that the classification scheme used for sorting is on target. One further step involves separating good and bad incidents, or rank-ordering incidents in terms of degree of effect (from very ineffective to very effective). Again, multiple raters should be used to reach a consensus on the importance of different behaviors.

6. Interpret and report the conclusions. Descriptive labels should be applied to each group of incidents. The list of categories reveals the major topical areas that should be covered in the training and performed on the job. By comparing the good and bad behaviors in each category, a profile of performance competencies can be created.

Special Application: Focus Groups and Nominal Group Technique

Another special kind of interviewing technique is the focus group and its cousin, the nominal group technique. Although the focus group procedure is borrowed from marketing, HRD practitioners will be familiar with such analogous processes as problem-solving teams, employee sensing or input forums, and the like. A *focus group* is a structured interview program with a group of people. A focus group interview provides information that helps one understand what people are thinking, how they might react to something, and their preferences for action (Krueger, 1988). In part, this means discovering the range of opinions that may exist on some topic. Focus groups can be particularly valuable for needs assessment.

The challenge in conducting focus groups is that the opinions of participants may be quite diverse, creating potential problems in eliciting widespread and complete disclosure during the interview. Such a reaction might occur if some people with divergent views felt overwhelmed by a strong majority view. This makes it important to create a permissive, nonthreatening atmosphere by establishing clear ground rules about participation at the start and managing the meeting so that everyone can express his or her views in turn.

The group should range in size from a minimum of 4 to a maximum of 12 to 15 participants, with an optimum size of around 7 to 10. Although group members may be strangers, a similar, homogeneous background is typically desirable to aid in analysis of the data. So, for example, if you were collecting information from managers and supervisors about a proposed training program, an initial consideration might be to include staff managers in one group and field managers in a second. Avoid putting a boss and a subordinate who reports directly to that boss in the same group.

The facilitator running the focus group should develop and follow a semistructured interview guide (called a questioning route). To develop the interview guide, one should do the following:

1. Define the purpose for the focus group clearly and specifically by answering such questions as, What kind of information is needed? What specific questions should be answered?

2. Brainstorm a long list of possible questions, which should then be narrowed down to a final list of no more than 10 questions, with 5 to 6 questions being optimum.

3. Make sure the questions are open-ended. For example: What was your reaction to the new product changes? Where do you obtain assistance in completing the new procedure? When do you provide employees feedback? How can we provide you with better information?

4. Arrange the questions logically, then pilot test the procedure. Modify the questions so that there is little confusion about what information you want.

The interviewer is really a moderator or facilitator of the discussion and should avoid expressing personal opinions on the subject. At the start of the group meeting, state the purpose and background of the study, identify the sponsor of the study, and indicate how the information obtained from the meeting will be used. The procedure to be followed should also be presented. Often, participants will be told that several questions will be asked, that they will have a moment to compose their views, and that others should not interrupt the person speaking. Since the discussion should be recorded with both a tape recorder and written notes, explain what will happen and be sure that the recorder is in plain view. The written notes should be good enough to replace a damaged tape.

The data are analyzed by looking for themes or recurring points of view. For each question, group the raw data by important categories, such as tenure, age, or position. Summarize each person's comments to each question. At this point, verbatim quotes are not as critical as identifying the essential meanings of each person's response. Look for key phrases, themes, issues, feelings, and so forth.

I use focus groups of managers to develop or redesign performance management and appraisal systems for client firms. Working with the human resources director, a group of approximately eight managers is invited to attend an initial planning meeting, which is conducted as a focus group to identify what problems managers experience with their current procedures, what changes they would like to see, and how a new system should be structured.

A slightly different form of group interview is the *nominal group technique* (NGT). NGT is similar to the Delphi method, in that both methods conduct a controlled brainstorming and critiquing process on some topic of interest. Thus, the basic procedures of the Delphi method—questioning rounds, brainstorming responses, summarizing responses, and providing feedback to the group—apply to NGT as well. However, for NGT, the process is carried out during one meeting with an assembled group. Rather than using the mail, the entire process is telescoped into a session lasting an hour or so.

■ Analyzing the Data

Once data are collected, the job is still not finished. Mounds of completed surveys, lists of test scores, reams of interview data, recordings of focus group discussions, and so forth are of little value unless all the information is put into summaries that are useful to planning, development, and evaluation. This stage of the research process is called *data analysis* (Rubin & Rubin, 1995).

In general, the purpose of analysis in applied HRD research is to group the information collected into categories that suggest what kinds of actions should be taken. For example, after interviewing 50 managers, what specific skills domains for training are indicated? What is the typical reading level of participants in a safety management program? How many trainees used what kinds of skills learned in a training program when they went back to the job? These and similar questions can be answered by analyzing the data.

Data analysis for applied HRD purposes involves three main steps: grouping similar data into categories, comparing the categories, and forming conclusions based on that comparison. Because the information will be used in planning or evaluating a HRD program, the analysis should be concise and easy to interpret. Data should be displayed in easy-to-follow tables, charts, or graphs.

1. *Grouping data into categories.* For standardized surveys, data are collected by category (e.g., "rate how good is the performance feedback you receive from your boss: excellent, good, satisfactory, fair, poor"), so this step is already accomplished. For other data, such as those collected through focus groups, observations, or interviews, there are long lists of raw information that await categorization. In these cases, the researcher must sift through all the commentary, looking for themes or characteristics that distinguish subsets of data.

   If there is no existing set of categories for grouping data, select some number of interviews, reports, observational checklists, or whatever other sort of data exists, to read through. As you read, look for common themes, and as they emerge, collect those themes into defined categories. Keep looking through this initial set of data until no new categories emerge. These newly formed categories become the general scheme for classifying the remaining data. Now, go through the remaining data, using symbols or notation to label or code each item into a category. Assemble each item into the classification system you have devised (Rubin & Rubin, 1995). For example, in looking through critical incident and observational reports of supervisory coaching practices, several categories might emerge: supportiveness and attention, knowledge of procedure, building self-confidence, constructive feedback, and instruction. Each critical incident and bit of observational data would be coded into one category. Then, in what could be a literal cut-and-paste operation, all of the data coded as dealing with supportiveness and attention would be assembled together, as would all the data relating to knowledge of procedure, and so forth. By grouping the data into categories, the meaning of each category can be established and the relative frequency or intensity of factors in each category identified.[1]

   If several coders are used, have them *independently* code and classify the same data. By comparing what percent of the total data is put in the same category, you have an estimate of how strong and reliable your coding system is. The net result of all this coding is to place most, if not all, of the data into categories that are meaningful and useful for the decisions to be made.

2. *Comparing the categories.* Once the categories are fleshed out, appropriate comparisons between categories can be made. What relationships exist between the categories? For example, continuing with the coaching example, do certain categories seem to go together, as might supportiveness and constructive feed-

back? Do certain categories vary independently or in opposition? Does knowledge have anything to do with building self-esteem? Does one category seem to produce, influence, or cause another, as one might expect between knowledge of a procedure and the amount or quality of instruction provided?

3. *Reaching conclusions.* The *conclusions* are the interpretations you draw from the data that have been categorized and compared. For coaching, one conclusion might be that the coach's amount of knowledge about a procedure directly affects the amount of time the coach spends coaching another person. The conclusions are verbalized statements of the data.

■ Reporting Research Results

Some research is used as soon as it is produced. As will be reviewed in Chapter 6, on preparing HRD solutions, studies of participant reading levels or entry motivation are consumed directly as part of the program design process. A summary of the results may not be necessary. Otherwise, if the research is complex or will be given to others for use, it is generally advisable to summarize the results of the research in a report. When the research used for an HRD program may affect employees, for example, in the form of passing or failing a program, a written report is strongly advised. Finally, the discipline of writing a report may force researchers to further clarify their interpretations and justifications, thereby strengthening the entire process.

The research report does not have to be long or abstract. On the contrary, the shorter and more precise the report, the better. Regardless of the length, though, the report should be professionally presented and structured for easy review and quick comprehension. To accomplish these goals, the following guidelines for report writing are offered.

1. Use a title page that includes a descriptive title of the study, the authors' names, to whom the report is presented, and the date.

2. Prepare an executive summary for the next page. This summary capsulizes the purpose of the study, how it was conducted, and its results. This should all fit on one page.

3. Use distinctive subheadings to signal and identify the main sections of the report: purpose or rationale, research procedure(s) used, characteristics of the people studied, findings and results, conclusions, and recommendations.

4. The data should be presented in clearly labeled charts, tables, and graphs. This information may be presented in appendices at the end of the report.

5. If the report will go to others, it would be a good idea to have colleagues read a draft of the report for comments and corrections before the report is sent.

CHART 3.1 Research in Employee Training and Development: Integrating Data Collection Methods with Stages of HRD Research

	Front-End Assessment					Developing HRD Solutions			Evaluation	
	Organizational Assessment	Performance Probability Analysis	Trainee Assessment	Readiness for Change	Competency Profile	Learner Characteristic	Program Materials	Pilot Review	Formative	Summative
Tests		X		X		X		X	X	X
Achievement		X	X							X
Learning		X	X			X				X
Surveys	X	X	X	X	X	X	X	X	X	X
Delphi	X		X		X					
Interviews		X	X		X	X	X	X	X	
Critical incident technique			X	X	X		X			X
Focus groups	X	X	X	X			X		X	X
Nominal group technique	X						X			
Observation	X	X	X		X			X	X	X
Rating scales			X							
Work samples			X		X					

NOTE: X = likely uses.

Remember, the report should be clear and concise. The text should specifically indicate the answers and recommendations needed by the organization.

■ Summary

The core task of research is collecting information. To this end, the HRD practitioner has a large and varied tool kit of methods and procedures for collecting data. Four principal methods have been reviewed: tests, direct observation, survey questionnaires, and interviews. For each generic method, there are derivative and specialized techniques.

These techniques provide the researcher with the "how-to" details and procedures for gathering information driven by research questions and needs. However, these methods are all form and protocol and do not by themselves indicate who or what should be tested, observed, surveyed, or interviewed. The practitioner must be able to apply these methods to the specific concerns associated with a HRD program. Knowing what kind of information to collect is also necessary, because this factor determines the substance of the research or what is specifically to be studied. This question—"what kind of information should be collected?"—is the focus of the remaining chapters. A framework for implementing these data collection techniques in relationship to the major steps of the HRD research process is shown in Chart 3.1.

■ Note

1. The creation of data categories and the display of data for easy use go hand-in-hand. Miles and Huberman (1984) provide a wealth of examples and guidance for how to convert qualitative data into useful charts, tables, and graphs.

4

FRONT-END ASSESSMENT

Identifying Performance Problems and Training Needs

■

Assume that you are a high-priced HRD consultant. One day, unexpectedly, you are offered a $500,000 contract to provide HRD programming. In that situation, you might have two questions. First, where is the check? Second, what kind of HRD programming must you provide? This second question forms the basis for the initial phase of HRD research: identifying performance problems that can be addressed through HRD interventions. What the various HRD research activities reviewed in Chapters 4 and 5 share is a common interest in identifying whether and how training is an appropriate response to concerns about performance.

Performance problems are identified using a discrepancy or gap model of performance (Kaufman & Thomas, 1980; Provus, 1971; Rothwell & Kazanas, 1992; Trimby, 1979). A training solution is appropriate when current performance is less than the level of performance expected or desired, especially when the reason for this performance shortfall is an insufficient level of knowledge or skills among the people from whom higher performance is expected. These research procedures compare current conditions against some standard to detect whether training is warranted.

Discrepancies between expected and actual performance may arise in several ways (Miller, Heiman, & Tuleja, 1985; Witkin, 1984). First, a new or transferred employee may not possess the skills needed to do the job. Second, the expectations for the job may change with new job duties or performance goals, new products or services, new customers, or new compliance requirements. Third, even if the job is not changing and there are no problems with current skills, technology and procedures may change, creating a need to learn new skills to perform more effectively. Regardless of the reason, in all of these cases, new expectations for job performance are being applied for which the performers are not prepared.

There are three important uses for the performance discrepancy model. First, be ready to independently examine a manager's or client's claims about the need for training. Line managers, pressured to meet performance goals, often jump to the conclusion that employee training will solve performance problems when in fact there can be any number of reasons for poor performance, including factors unrelated to knowledge or skills deficiencies. A good analysis of performance problems can identify which solution—training or some other sort of intervention—is best. Second, a good analysis is essential for effective program evaluation. A clear statement of the performance problem indicates what should be improved by the training intervention. As a result, program effects and results can be evaluated directly. Third, with this model, one can assume a proactive approach to HRD administration. That is, one does not need to wait for performance problems to be noted by others. One can create a continuous "surveillance" system monitoring performance indicators that will identify current or future problems in one's organization (Smith, Delahaye, & Gates, 1986). For example, changes in job duties can be anticipated, so a future-oriented or strategic job analysis can be used (Schneider & Konz, 1989).

■ Training "Needs" Assessment

The traditional approach to performance problems has been to base program planning on the "needs" of the trainees (Nadler, 1982). Needs assessment is the research procedure usually recommended for this phase of HRD planning. A training needs assessment (TNA) is intended to systematically identify training needs to set priorities for the training and properly allocate resources (e.g., money, time) (Witkin, 1984). A *need* is generally understood to be a discrepancy between desired and actual performance. Training needs *assessment* should, therefore, gather data on both expected and actual performance, then compare the two to reveal discrepancies. A training needs *analysis* looks for the causes of any discrepancies that are found. Assessment must precede analysis (Benjamin, 1989; Kaufman & Valentine, 1989).

However, the traditional approach to needs assessment has three problems. First, need is not well defined. Educational and training needs have been described in different ways (Trimby, 1979). For example, needs may mean biological drives, cognitively defined wants or demands, or normative educational prescriptions (Atwood & Ellis, 1971; Conner, Jacobi, Altman, & Aslanian, 1985; James, 1956). Needs could either be basic (physiological) or felt (described by the person as important) (Scissons, 1982). The lack of a clearly defined and generally accepted meaning of *need* has prompted some to suggest simply dropping its use in educational and training planning (Mattimore-Knudson, 1983; Rossett, 1990). Others suggest that the idea of a *need* be replaced by the more interesting concept of *training demand,* which would include both willingness and commitment to participate in program offerings (Mitchell & Hyde, 1979).

Second, due in part to the confusion over defining *need,* there is no universal model of TNA (Witkin, 1984). For example, models of TNA often take the form of lists of data collection techniques but neglect to suggest what kind of data should be collected (Nowack, 1991; Smith et al., 1986; Steadman, 1980). Although these approaches are perfectly acceptable on their own terms, they lack a larger framework for positioning and supporting HRD planning. Traditional approaches to needs assessment tend to focus on either the competence discrepancies or stated training preferences of each individual learner, while ignoring the larger context in which performance occurs. Thus, TNA might be conducted on topics of marginal value to the larger organization (e.g., on how well employees "dress for success") and not connect with issues of much greater concern, such as sales or quality.

Third, by concentrating on individual learning "needs," traditional approaches to TNA may completely ignore larger issues, such as whether training is the right solution for the performance problem in question or how well the training will transfer back to the job. Both issues should be critical to planning HRD programs. If a performance problem is due to faulty work processes or motivational conditions, no amount of training will make a difference. Likewise, even the best training will be of little value if there are barriers on the job that inhibit or prevent using what was learned.

Thus, although the traditional needs assessment approach recognizes the importance of basing training on discrepancies between expected and actual performance, the approach is beset by lingering problems. The solution is to broaden and extend the research horizon beyond this concern with discrepancies in individual performance. In short, a process of *front-end assessment* is indicated. Such a process embeds the focus on identifying learner competency "needs" within a larger framework of identifying important organizational performance problems; considering the entire set of forces, either skills or otherwise, that may be producing the problems; and evaluating whether and how training will work on the job.

■ Improving on TNA: Front-End Assessment

The front-end assessment process advocated here includes four different research procedures. The purpose of these research procedures is to provide answers to the critical issues involved in considering and planning a training intervention. Those issues are captured by these four questions:

1. Is there a performance problem?
2. To what extent is the source of the performance problem due to ability deficiencies or to other systemic causes?
3. Who needs what kind of training?
4. What barriers may exist to prevent the training from being effective?

Effective HRD planning depends on finding answers to all these questions. In some situations, the answers may be obvious and not require any research. For example, planned changes in products, technologies, or job duties may be so apparent that questions 1, 2, and 3 can be answered without further study. However, if the answers are not clear or obvious, research and investigation should be carried out.

There are four main domains, then, in which a front-end assessment can be conducted. These domains correspond to the four questions just noted and are shown in Figure 4.1. An *organizational assessment* seeks to identify the performance discrepancies that exist in the organization. Four methods and techniques for organizational assessment are reviewed in this chapter.

A *performance problem analysis* examines the extent to which the discrepancy is due to learning and skills deficits or to other systemic factors. This kind

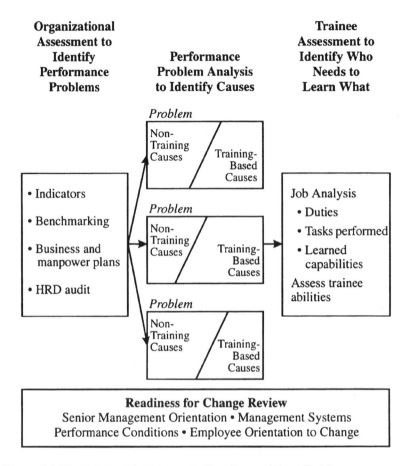

Figure 4.1. The Relationship Between the Four Types of Front-End Assessment

of analysis, covered in Chapter 5, investigates the various reasons for perform-ance problems.

Chapter 5 continues by addressing the more traditional focus of needs assessment. Given a list of required job knowledge and skills, a *trainee assess-ment* seeks to learn what specific abilities must be taught to whom through HRD activities. A *readiness for change* review considers what barriers may exist to prevent the transfer of the training to the job and the adoption of the change inside the operating system. This review is also covered in Chapter 5. Depending on the circumstances, the HRD practitioner may not need to do all four studies. Regardless of which research projects are selected, though, the researcher should develop a research plan that outlines what the study is and how it will be conducted. See again Chart 2.1 for an example of what a research plan should cover.

■ Organizational Assessment

An *organizational assessment* searches for key problems in overall organizational performance. Problems may be detected in a variety of realms, including the financial, marketing, quality, service, strategic, operational, or human resources areas. A problem may exist because the organization's performance is below that of its competitors or because there is an unsatisfactory discrepancy between performance expectations and performance results. This form of research also looks for answers to the question of whether there are performance problems at an aggregated, organizational level (which may mean the company as a whole; plants, divisions, or regional operations; or specific departments, units, or branches within a single organization). In this context, there are four techniques available for identifying performance problems. The techniques are tracking performance indicators, benchmarking, business and human resources planning, and auditing the HRD function.

Tracking Indicators of Organizational Performance

Indicators of organizational performance can be any aggregate measure of input, efficiency, output, or organizational effectiveness. Certainly, financial measures of revenue, cost, or profitability, or ratios based on those measures (such as return on sales), provide windows for viewing how well the organization is doing in any number of performance areas. Other indicators may include measures of product sales or quality, customer satisfaction, or human resources use, such as turnover, productivity, attendance, or employee commitment (Rothwell & Kazanas, 1989). These indicators can be compared to themselves over time (are sales increasing or decreasing?) or to similar indicators compiled into industry averages. For example, various reports, often available at public libraries, can provide industry averages for financial indicators.[1] In addition, indicators can be tracked in terms of all managers (e.g., annual turnover of each departmental manager) or by office or store (e.g., quarterly sales by branch), thereby facilitating performance comparisons between units or managers inside the organization.

Since this information was collected by others for uses apart from your research purposes, it may be a good idea to assay the quality of the information. Look for any problems with the information that make it suspect by looking at the circumstances under which the data were collected. Was there any aspect of data collection that might raise questions about their accuracy and value? For example, employee opinion surveys that were returned directly to the employee's supervisor without any privacy protections suggest an obvious problem, especially if the results were uniformly glowing. Other questions to consider include the following:

1. How old are the data? For specific organizational problems, the older the data, the less chance that they are still relevant and meaningful. I once was asked to put together a communications training program for a group of managers who scored low on communications in an employee opinion survey. Unfortunately, the data were more than a year old, and much had changed since that time.

2. If the data were derived from a sample, was the sample sufficiently large and representative of the larger population? How was the sample selected? If a sample of employees was used, consider how that sample was formed. The most important issue is random selection: If the sample was picked randomly, a small size may be acceptable. If not, then the sample should be large, in the best case, representing at least half of the total population.

A convenient way to analyze such information is to use the PIP, or Potential for Improving Performance (Gilbert, 1978). The PIP looks at the difference between exemplary and average performance on some measure of organizational performance. To complete a PIP analysis, two pieces of information are needed. One is a measure of exemplary performance; this does not have to be the highest level of performance ever reached but should be the highest sustainable level of performance. The other is a measure of the average performance for all units included in the set of data. Since raw performance numbers may mask differences in extraneous factors affecting performance (such as size of the sales territory or local economic conditions), it is preferable to normalize the measures, that is, to reduce them to some common denominator. Consider a corporation with 10 different widget manufacturing plants. Rather than just compare the number of widgets made at each plant (which may vary by the size of workforce), it would be better to compute widget productivity for each plant. This can be calculated fairly easily by dividing the number of widgets produced (each day, each month, or by whatever production cycle makes sense) by some measure of labor input, such as the number of employees. The resulting per-plant productivity number gives a much better basis of comparison (Brethower, 1994).

The PIP score is calculated by dividing the exemplary measure by the average measure. The higher the PIP score, the more variance or range there is in performance—and the more opportunity there is for improving performance. PIPs of 1.5 or higher are strong candidates for intervention (Zemke & Kramlinger, 1982). Continuing with the widget example, assume that the best plant productivity averages 525 widgets per day, whereas the productivity average for all 10 plants is, say, 275. The resulting PIP of 1.9 (525/275) indicates that there is an opportunity to almost double the performance of the entire system if all the remaining plants were to perform as productively as the best performer.

PIPs may be computed in other ways, too (Zemke & Kramlinger, 1982). For example, if the original PIP is low, finer analysis may still point to performance problems. Rather than comparing the exemplar with the group average, one could compare the average for the lowest 10%, 20%, or 25% of performers against either the group average or the average of the corresponding highest 10%, 20%, or 25%. Say another firm, also making widgets, has a PIP of 1.4. However, the widget production average for the lowest 20% of performers is 375, whereas that for the top 20% is 619. By recomputing the PIP using these two as comparison, a PIP of 1.65 emerges.

Benchmarking

A second method for identifying performance problems is *benchmarking*. Popularized by Xerox in the 1980s and then swept up by the quality management movement (Ford, 1993; Main, 1992), benchmarking is a method for comparing an organizational process—such as accounts payable, product development, or a manufacturing procedure—against that process in another organization. The process used as the basis for comparison must be identified as a superior one. In effect, in a benchmarking study, one's own process is evaluated against a similar process that is considered the best in its class. Based on this comparison, problems with the organization's processes are highlighted. Using a benchmarking approach, Ford compared its accounts payable function, which required 500 employees, to Mazda's, which needed fewer than 10. Further analysis led to changes in procedures and the reduction of Ford's staff to 200 (Main, 1992).

A benchmarking project begins by identifying what process to study. Any organizational process with the following characteristics should be marked with a red flag to indicate that it is a prime candidate for a benchmarking study: The process is vital to overall organizational performance, there are problems in production or delivery, and it involves significant cost. Once the process is selected, describe in detail how the process is carried out in your organization. This can be done with workflow diagrams, procedure lists, task statements, and the like (Camp, 1989). At the same time, some common unit of measurement (such as unit cost, customer satisfaction, or employee productivity) should be selected and gauged.

The second step is to identify a benchmarking partner for comparison. There are several possible sources: other operations inside your organization, direct competitors, industry leaders, or general exemplars. For example, a mail-order operation (such as music CDs) might select the L. L. Bean (clothing) catalogue business to study. Top performers may be spotted in reports from the business or functional (accounting, R&D, manufacturing, etc.) press, or from trade associations. Best performers may also be identified from information published by the company itself.

The benchmarking candidate is then asked to participate in the study. Seek referrals or introductions from ex-employees, suppliers, consultants, professional acquaintances, business associations, and the like. The request to participate can be made more interesting by promising to avoid areas in which there might be restraint of trade problems and to avoid proprietary matters; by guaranteeing confidentiality and that the information will not be shared with outside parties unless the partner first agrees; and by being willing to share comparable internal information about your internal processes (Fitz-enz, 1993).

An on-site visit to the comparison organization is essential. Several personnel from your organization should participate, including the person responsible for the process being studied. The visit should be planned so that both an observation and an interview guide are prepared. Provide the comparison company with an agenda of the visit in advance. After the meeting, debrief participants on what was learned, preparing a thorough summary of findings. With this information, the comparison can begin. Look for sources of competitive problems that may be due to operational procedure factors, management factors (such as compensation, training, etc.), or geographic or workplace structural problems. Then make plans for correcting these problems. Training is one important, expected solution to competitive problems.

Benchmarking can be used to evaluate a firm's HRM practices (Schneier & Johnson, 1993). For example, an organization's human resources—its people—are an increasingly important source of competitive advantage. The selection, compensation, and training systems used by an organization either add to, maintain, or detract from the value of those human resources. Pfeffer (1994) suggests that an organization can benchmark its own HRM practices against the criteria used by the Malcolm Baldrige National Quality Award. Of a possible total of 1,000 points, up to 250 points can be earned in the categories of human resources use and leadership. The standards used by the Baldrige Award to evaluate candidates in these categories represent a best practices list that can easily be used in a benchmarking study.

Human Resources and Business Planning

Both business and human resources plans can be used to identify potential problems in organizational performance. Business plans that call for shifts in strategic direction, new technology, new products, new sales, or new service delivery systems should serve as baselines for anticipating future performance problems. As a result, business plans should be used as a framework for identifying what kinds of talent (skills and capabilities) the organization will need to accomplish the desired results. Human resources plans project the supply of trained talent in the organization against a forecasted demand for that same talent (Walker, 1980). Projected shortfalls in the supply of talent signal potential performance problems.

Auditing the HRD Function

Auditing is the independent evaluation of the soundness and effectiveness of an organization's system of control over ongoing operations meant to assess any risks in those operations (Wallace, 1991). Controls include those processes used to safeguard assets, to make assets available on a timely basis, and to discover any errors or irregularities in operational administration. To the extent that risks are not controlled, the organization is exposed to the possibility of loss of assets due to theft, negligence, or malfeasance. Traditionally, auditing has focused on a company's financial assets to verify the accuracy of its financial statements. To make their judgments, auditors use a normative model of control that depicts how activities should be conducted. A financial auditor uses, for example, a normative model about how financial transactions flowing through a bookkeeping department should be recorded, processed, and reported. After comparing what practices *are* being used in the bookkeeping department with this model of how they *should* be done, the auditor will judge a system to be either satisfactory, qualified (some exceptions to satisfactory), or unsatisfactory (Chelimsky, 1985; Wallace, 1991).

Increasingly, the auditing function is being repositioned as a method for examining the risks in a variety of different operations and practices, including human resources. In this context, risks do not have to be exclusively or directly financial. For example, Hills and Bergman (1987) show how to conduct an "equal pay for equal work audit." In this audit procedure, all employees in a particular job category, such as "service representative," are identified in terms of average salary, recent performance appraisals, and pay adjustments. The pay treatment of men and women is then compared to detect potential discriminatory compensation practices. The Office of Federal Contract Compliance Programs (Kelly, 1993; U.S. Department of Labor, 1991) focuses a significant portion of one chapter of its compliance manual on how to audit management and organizational practices that may create a "glass ceiling" (a barrier to the movement of women and minorities into senior management positions). Other applications of auditing to HRM practices include auditing human resources planning and development systems (Burack, 1988; Burack & Mathys, 1980), employment practices (Lewis, 1992), performance appraisals (Burchett & De Meuse, 1985), payroll systems (Arens & Loebbecke, 1984), and human resources information system data (Myers-Goodman, 1990). In each of these cases, there is potential for either real, direct, or potentially indirect losses to the organization from poorly controlled human resources practices.

In the same vein, the HRD function of an organization can—and in some cases, should—be audited. Here, HRD is intentionally referred to as a "function" rather than a department because an HRD audit should be carried out regardless of whether or not a specific training department exists. An HRD audit should concentrate on the risks involved in training administration and operations. However, a major question at this stage is who should do the audit. Presumably, an audit is done by someone independent of the operation being audited. However, because an HRD audit has little if any legal standing at this time, the independence issue may be less critical. The value of the audit comes from nipping potential problems in the bud before they blossom into full-scale crises. Practitioners involved with an HRD function may wish to conduct their own internal audits in preparation for or in lieu of more formal audits.

As in any audit, administrative records of HRD operations and practices should be searched to determine if there are any significant areas of risk. Likewise, the methods used for collecting information for records (such as program registration lists or graduation test scores) should also be studied. In some cases, the auditor should test the accuracy of records and controls by collecting additional evidence. For example, interviews with disabled trainees would identify any problems with reasonable accommodation, inspection of training manuals would reveal whether certain topics (such as how to conduct a legal hiring interview) are covered, and survey forms asking about safety training received would indicate whether the training was actually conducted as presented. A file of the evidence and other supporting materials (called the *working papers*) should be kept (Wallace, 1991).

Risks can be associated with HRD in several areas of administration and operations, including fair employment compliance, safety training, and management negligence. In effect, each of these areas has prescribed or normative models of HRD practices.

Fair Employment Compliance

Like other employment practices, training activities are covered by various civil rights laws. This means that employees who believe that they are being discriminated against in training have as much legal standing as if they felt mistreated in hiring or compensation practices. Therefore, the administration of HRD programs should be examined for any potential discriminatory effects. There are several specific areas that require attention.

a. *Trainee selection.* Are women, minorities, or members of other protected groups being excluded from training in a disproportionate number?

b. *Treatment of trainees.* Does training adversely discriminate against certain classes of people? If so, can the basis of the discrimination be justified? For example, consider a training program that relies exclusively on materials printed in English and in which nonnative-born participants tend to be less successful in the training than native-born trainees. If the training was for librarians, for whom facility with English would be essential to job performance, the nature of the training and any subsequent negative effects would be more defensible than if the training was for a nonskilled laborer's position, where English language proficiency would not be so essential.[2]

c. *Adverse impact on trainees from training results.* If the results of participation in a training program are used to make personnel decisions (such as hiring, promotion, or termination), are women, minorities, or other protected individuals being disproportionately and adversely affected (Bartlett, 1978; Wiesen, 1987)? If training results are so used, the evaluation and assessment procedures (testing, assessments, reports, etc.) are subject to challenge with regard to their validity, reliability, and fairness. Is there sufficient and appropriate documentation behind the tests to withstand challenges to their technical adequacy?[3]

d. *Adverse effect on others from training results.* Did the training lead to any unfair employment practices among others indirectly affected by the training? For example, one of my client firms completed an adverse impact study of employee appraisal ratings after all of the firm's supervisors completed a performance appraisal training program. Employee ratings were grouped by white and minority, and by male and female, to determine if any de facto discrimination resulted from the program. (None did.) The worksheet used in this analysis is shown in Table 4.1.

TABLE 4.1 Adverse Impact Assessment of Employee Appraisal Ratings

	Appraisal Ratings				
	Outstanding	Exceeds Expectations	Meets Expectations	Not Acceptable	Does Not Meet Expectations
Men (total)	2	22	26	6	1
White		20	19	4	1
Black	1	1	4	2	
Hispanic		1			
Asian	1		3		
Native American					
Women (total)	11	74	91	12	3
White	9	52	58	6	1
Black	2	21	32	6	2
Hispanic			1		
Asian					
Native American					

NOTE: Data represent the final summary appraisal rating given to 248 employees in a financial institution. All appraisals were completed in December 1991.

e. *Records retention.* Records covering all of the issues previously noted should be kept. Recordkeeping requirements vary by law and employer size, so presenting universal rules about what to keep and for how long is not possible here. Check with specific regulations or legal counsel for advice.

Required Training

Various laws may *require* employee training. This is particularly true in the area of on-the-job safety (OSHA, 1992b). Otherwise, as will be discussed more fully in the next section, training is a prudent (but not mandated) step for avoiding risks in other areas of employment practice.

Perhaps the best-known safety training requirements are the Hazardous Chemicals Communications standards (or HazCom) (OSHA, 1991, 1992a). As part of these standards, employers are obligated to inform employees about any hazardous chemicals in the workplace and to prepare (or train) them in how to protect themselves from these chemicals. Other OSHA regulations place safety training requirements on employers, depending on the industry and the nature of the work. For example, employers may be required to provide training in each of the following areas: personal protective equipment, fire protection, first aid, and electrical work practices. A related area in which training may be required stems from the Drug-free Workplace Act: Some employers are required to provide education to their employees about drugs (Ledvinka & Scarpello, 1992).

Failure to provide required training increases the health risks to employees, and failure to keep suitable records of the training provided increases the liability risks to employers. An important step in auditing safety matters is to first identify all the potential training requirements covering businesses in your industry and then to assess the extent to which training in those areas is being provided by your company. If the audit turns up deficiencies, corrective action should be undertaken (Tompkins, 1993).

Management Negligence

Developments in the field of HRM have increased the accountability of organizations for training employees and their managers. Harmful results that can be determined to have arisen from inadequate training of employees can lead to litigation. Management action or inaction that reveals carelessness or thoughtlessness about employee training and development may be labeled *negligent* and treated accordingly by the courts.

There are several "hot button" cases in which management action or inaction might be particularly subject to claims of negligence. In these cases, training programs are not specifically mandated or required. However, lack of appropriate training can contribute to an onset of problems and could serve as evidence of management negligence. Consider, for example, sexual harassment. Laws and regulations define it and make it illegal. To avoid sexual harassment lawsuits, a prudent employer should make sure all supervisors are trained in what to do or not to do with regard to this issue.[4] In addition, supervisors might be tested, nonpunitively, on their knowledge of discrimination and diversity issues. Attitudinal surveys of the management team could indicate any deep-seated racist, sexist, or other such attitudes that could lead to problems down the road ("Pregnancy Discrimination," 1995).

Another area of concern is that of employee benefits, especially 401(k) retirement plans (Johnson, 1996). The growing popularity of 401(k) plans has brought increasing risk for plans without sufficient variety in investment options and, of note here, inadequate employee education. Although employees direct their own investments, risk arises if the employees' investments lose value or don't make what the employees were led to believe they could make. Employers offering such plans face the challenge of making sure employees receive sufficient training to make informed decisions while also managing to avoid providing investment advice. Without proper training in this area, an organization may face unnecessary risk.

Supervisory training in the following areas would also help reduce the risk of adverse fallout: writing performance appraisals, carrying out hiring interview procedures, administering company personnel policies, and dealing with potentially violent employees. Along the same lines, are employees being properly trained to do their jobs? I was once called for a deposition in a case in which a customer of the bank for which I had been working claimed loss of deposits because of teller negligence. In this case, the teller worked in an outlying region where we did not provide the regular teller training program. According to the customer, it was the lack of training that caused the problem. (The issue was settled out of court.)

Finally, one emerging area of potential HRD risk and liability involves so-called "new age" training (Miller & Abramson, 1987). Such programs use novel training techniques as part of a specific value agenda. Employees may think these programs force religious conversion and object accordingly. Similar problems have been noted in diversity training programs. For example, one FAA employee sued because, while attending a required diversity training program, he had to walk through a gauntlet of jeering female employees in a manner reminiscent of the U.S. Navy's Tailhook scandal (Marbella, 1994).

The Audit Procedure

An effective audit requires careful and thorough planning. For HRD audit purposes, planning should focus on the preparation of an appropriate audit guide. Essentially, the guide is a checklist of all the items to be audited. For each item, three rating categories are possible: satisfactory, qualified (some exceptions to satisfactory), or unsatisfactory. Items may be grouped together into sections (such as the three categories of risk noted earlier). There should also be room after each item or section to write comments, problems observed, or recommendations.

The audit should include all potential areas of HRD risk facing the operation. For example, any required training, such as for hazardous chemicals or a drug-free workplace, should be inspected. Based on the nature of the business and industry, other training may also be either required or recommended. The HRD researcher *qua* auditor should include all other items that are indicated. The items should be clearly stated and defined. In addition, it may be necessary to list and inspect specific elements of each item. Consider hazardous chemicals

CHART 4.1 Template of HRD Audit Guide

Required Training
1. Hazardous chemicals (HazCom)

	Satisfactory	Qualified	Unsatisfactory
a. Is HazCom training provided?	☐	☐	☐
b. Are all employees covered by the requirement included in the training?	☐	☐	☐
c. Is the training conducted in a timely manner?	☐	☐	☐
d. Does the training adequately cover the necessary material?	☐	☐	☐
Comments _____			

training: Specific elements to check would include provision, coverage, timing, and adequacy. Chart 4.1 provides a template for the audit guide.

When conducting the audit, you should plan to inspect and study procedures and materials; don't rely on only your own memory or others' reports. Look for files on each course and the training materials used in the course. Files should contain information about curriculum planning and development, course announcements, selection procedures, attendance, evaluations, and any follow-up actions taken. The procedures in place for producing and maintaining those files should also be examined. Make notes about any materials or procedures that may be problematic. Once the audit is complete, prepare a report that summarizes the findings. In the report, indicate what was audited and why, along with the ratings given. Point out any areas of concern or problems and suggest remedies. If you are auditing a HRD function as an outsider, you should discuss and review that report with the person responsible. If you are auditing a function for which you are responsible, you should be sure to take action to correct any problems identified by the audit.

Summary

All four of these organizational assessment procedures can be used to discover any areas of organizational performance in which there is a discrepancy from what is expected. These assessments can be carried out in response to requests for training. However, the HRD practitioner would be well advised to set up procedures for conducting these assessments on an ongoing basis. Such ongoing assessments act as regular X-rays taken of organization performance that allow the HRD practitioner to take a proactive stance in identifying potential performance problems. By focusing on important areas of organizational performance, HRD programs can produce important results.

■ Summary

The first step in applied HRD research is to identify performance problems for which HRD interventions are appropriate remedies. Traditionally, "needs assessment" has been the research step advocated for handling this process. Yet the traditional approach to needs assessment is weighted down by a lack of clarity about what *needs* really are. A better, more inclusive research approach is a front-end assessment. There are four primary forms of front-end assessment research.

The first form of front-end assessment, covered in this chapter, is the process of organizational assessment. Organizational assessment isolates those areas of performance that are critical to organizational success. Those areas are then measured against certain standards of performance to detect any areas needing improvement. Four research and analytic techniques for doing this were presented. First, indicators of financial, quality, service, or human resources performance can be compared, either over time or against an industry standard, to identify problems. A PIP analysis can establish the system's potential for performance improvements. Second, benchmarking studies can do much the same by comparing current practices against superior ones found in other organizations. Third, business or human resources plans can be examined for problems. Finally, an audit of the fairness, compliance, and due diligence of training functions may also root out problems worthy of attention.

An organizational assessment can play a critical role in the early stages of a front-end assessment by keeping the HRD practitioner's eye on the bigger picture and by positioning HRD interventions to address issues of great importance to the health and well-being of the organization. But are HRD interventions the right solutions for the problems found? If so, what kind of training intervention is needed? And how can the intervention be given the best chance to succeed? To these three questions—and to the three remaining research endeavors that are part of front-end assessment—we now turn in Chapter 5.

■ Notes

1. Dun and Bradstreet Information Services publishes a booklet called *Industry Norms and Key Business Ratios, Desktop Edition.* In it, average levels of performance on a variety of balance sheet accounts and for a number of operating ratios are listed by industry segment. For example, if one wanted to know the average return on assets for firms in Household Furniture Manufacturing (SIC code 251), that information would be available through this source. Such information provides a baseline for comparing an organization's performance against the averages for firms operating in the same industry.

2. See the section in Chapter 6 about training and disabled employees for further discussion on the issue of discriminatory treatment and training.

3. See Wiesen (1987) for a thorough review of the specific issues involved in auditing HRD program effects.

4. Some states require sexual harassment training, including Maine, Connecticut, Illinois, Tennessee, and Utah (Mathiason & Pierce, 1996).

5

FRONT-END ASSESSMENT

Training Programming
From Needs Assessment

■

Assume that you have conducted an organizational assessment as described in Chapter 4. Based on a comparison of performance indicators, benchmarking studies, an analysis of business plans, or an audit of the training function, you discover that revenue is off, that productivity is down, that market share is slipping, or that customers are not as satisfied with service as they should be. Clearly, these are signals that action is required. But what kind of action? Will a training program be sufficient to reverse these trends or should other actions be taken? If training is indicated, what should the program cover, and who should attend? Finally, remembering that what is learned in training may not always survive the trip back to the workplace, what can be done to give the HRD program the best chance of success? These questions frame the remaining steps of front-end assessment, which are discussed in turn in this chapter.

■ Performance Problem Analysis

After the identification of organizational performance problems, the key question is to what extent the problem arises because of insufficient abilities among the performers or because of other systemic causes. Of course, in the real world, one will seldom find performance problems caused by only skills deficiencies or another factor. Clark (1992) illustrates this point nicely.

> Assuming that the many organizational problems that can reduce or inhibit performance have been ruled out . . . training requirements exist only when employees have not yet learned to perform some aspect of a job and/or have low general ability. . . . The solution to most performance problems is most often some combination of clear communication of goals and expectations; accurate information about the task or job, often in the form of job aids . . . the opportunity to practice . . . and feedback (p. 697f)

In short, performance problems will typically have many sources. Discovering these sources is the task of performance problem analysis (Rosenberg, 1990).

There have been two popular approaches to performance problem analysis. Mager and Pipe (1970) provided an early approach. Following the routes of a decision-tree, the analyst uses a series of questions to determine the nature of the performance issue: Is the problem important? Is it due to a skill deficiency? If it is, then either training or practice is indicated. If it is not, look at the conditions under which the performance occurs: Is desired performance rewarded, ignored, or punished, and are there obstacles to performance? As is made obvious in this approach, poor performance may be due to skills deficiencies or to the behavioral contingencies and conditions present in the larger environment.

Gilbert (1978; Dean, 1994) expanded this approach by using a more detailed analytic map of the relevant performance characteristics of both the work environment and the individual performer. These characteristics are grouped under a behaviorist framework of stimuli, responses, and consequences. Gilbert (1982) integrated these elements into what he called a PROBE model of analysis. The model provides a series of questions that the analyst can use to isolate the origins of a performance problem. For example, the HRD practitioner should look at the following aspects of the work environment: for stimuli, how much information is available about performance expectations and feedback; for response characteristics, to what extent are technological, budgetary, and work resources available; and for consequences, what events (either reinforcing or punishing) follow performance? Individually, stimuli characteristics cover the amount of training provided; response characteristics cover the capacity of the person to perform; and consequences cover the motives of the performer to work for the incentives provided. Gilbert's model can be extended by considering other situational factors that shape work performance. Peters, O'Connor, and Rudolf (1980) list eight such factors, including job-related information, tools and equipment, materials, financial support, services and support, personal preparation, time, and physical comfort.

These approaches can be integrated into the following model (Clardy, 1985). This model serves as a checklist for conducting a performance problem analysis; it presumes that there may be any number of causes for a performance discrepancy, only some of which are due to skills deficiencies. In particular, this model identifies six sets of factors that can be used to explain the nature and level of performance observed.[1]

1. *Assignment of duties.* Do the employees know that they are expected to perform a duty or task? For example, in a total quality program, do employees know that they are expected to identify and recommend improvements?

2. *Standards of performance.* Does the employee know the level of performance that is expected? It is one thing to know that you are expected to recommend improvements and another to know if those recommendations are to be made as informal suggestions or formal, fully developed proposals with cost-benefit estimates.

3. *Work process.* Are the work procedures well designed and organized? Does the employee have access to an appropriate level of technology and equipment?

4. *Trained and willing.* Does the employee have the skills needed to perform the tasks as expected? Is the employee sufficiently motivated to perform?

5. *Consequences.* What happens when the employee performs? Is the employee rewarded, punished, or ignored?

6. *Feedback.* Do the employees receive information about their performance in a way that allows them to adjust and improve?

Table 5.1 summarizes this model and its performance management implications.

The HRD practitioner should conduct a performance problem analysis to understand what factors may be contributing to the problem. Essentially, the analyst is discovering if each factor is present in sufficient degree to support successful performance. By identifying which factors, if any, are in distress, the full range of appropriate interventions capable of bringing about a meaningful solution can be implemented. This approach acknowledges that training by itself is unlikely to be a sufficient solution to a performance problem.

An example of the importance of performance problem analysis comes from recent work I did with the customer service department of a small utility. An increase in customer complaints prompted the management team to ask me to provide customer service training. However, prior to the training, I carried out a performance problem analysis using a combination of interviews and observation. Based on this analysis, it became clear that deficiencies in customer

TABLE 5.1 Performance Factors: Breakdowns and Solutions

Factors	Breakdowns	Solutions
Assignment of duty	– Not defined as part of job	+ Make clear assignment
	– Unclear cues about when to act	+ Make cues known
Performance expectations	– Standards do not exist or are unknown	+ Establish and communicate standards
	– Standards are too high (never reached)	+ Modify
Work process	– Inadequate tools	+ Upgrade technology
	– Work process is convoluted	+ Streamline and simplify
	– Too many competing demands	+ Control interruptions
Worker skill and motivation	– Employee does not know how to do job	+ Train
	– Employee is not motivated	+ Change outcomes, counsel, replace
Consequences	– Desired performance is punished or ignored and nonperformance is rewarded	+ Change consequences so that desired performance is reinforced and undesired performance is not
	– Consequences are not clear	+ Specify nature of consequences
	– Consequences are unpredictable	+ Link specific consequences to performance
Feedback	– No information on performance given	+ Provide information
	– Feedback given is late, vague, confusing	+ Improve the quality of feedback

service skills were the least of the problems. Indeed, the current system violated virtually every factor of the performance model previously noted. First, the assignment of duties was unclear, especially in the matter of supervision. Ostensibly, all five of the customer service representatives (CSRs) reported to a division director, who was also responsible for finance, marketing, and human resources. With 12 direct reports, he told the CSRs not to bother him. Instead, one of the more tenured CSRs believed she was the de facto supervisor; her efforts at managing the others caused resentment and animosity. Second, there were no stated standards for serving the customers who came to pay their bills, open new accounts, or ask for service. Third, the layout of the service area invited difficult customer interactions: A short, open counter for handling all customer transactions meant any communication occurred in the full view of everyone else. The work processes were designed so that a person simply wanting to pay a bill might have to wait for an open window behind customers with complaints. As a result of these factors, the stress levels among the CSRs were high and motivation was low. There were seldom any positive consequences experienced at work, whereas punitive consequences seemed to occur with each new customer. Finally, there was no mechanism for assessing customer satisfaction or providing feedback on performance. The underlying roots of the customer service problem would not have been solved by providing only training.

The steps in carrying out a performance problem analysis are fairly straightforward. Typically, the researcher should plan to interview the performers in the system to assess their understanding of job duties and expectations and to gain an understanding of motivation factors and conditions, to interview management about expectations and management processes, and to observe work processes. The resulting analysis should list the six factors and identify to what extent each factor is present or absent. Recommendations should follow.

In summary, it is important to look for all of the causes behind performance problems. Rarely is training the only appropriate solution; instead, it is likely that a number of factors may need attention and a variety of solutions may need to be applied. A performance problem analysis, using the six-factor model presented here, can help locate all of the potential sources of difficulties and suggest the proper solutions.

■ Trainee Assessment

For problems in performance that seem to be due to skills deficiencies, HRD programs are indicated. The major issue confronting the analyst at this point is: What exactly do the performers need to learn? That is, given that a skills deficiency is apparent, what exactly is the nature of that deficiency? The answers to this question are addressed through a process of trainee assessment. Trainee assessment really includes two distinct but related steps: a job analysis to yield a list of skills for the job and an assessment of the degree to which the potential trainees possess the required knowledge and skills (Mirabile, Caldwell, & O'Reilly, 1987). Each will be reviewed in the following pages.

Job Analysis

If there are performance problems in sales, service, or productivity, the positions responsible for performance in these areas should be identified so that the job(s) can be analyzed. A *job analysis* involves defining the duties, tasks, and skills involved in the job identified from the performance problem analysis (Gael, 1983). For HRD research purposes, a job analysis involves three distinct steps (Goldstein, 1986). First, the duties of the job should be identified. Second, the tasks performed in completing those duties—and the conditions under which those duties are performed—should be described. Third, the knowledge and skills required to perform those tasks should be listed.

Identify Job Duties

If there are current, accurate job descriptions of the positions being reviewed, the first step of identifying job duties is done. If not, the analyst should undertake such an analysis. Job duties can be discovered in several ways: by observing incumbents in their jobs, by interviewing incumbents and their supervisors (often using some kind of Position Analysis Questionnaire; see McCormick, 1976), or by reviewing any available training or procedural materials. The analyst should seek to produce as inclusive and exhaustive a list of job duties as possible.

Once the list is developed, it should be turned into a survey questionnaire for distribution to the job incumbents. Depending on the size of the workforce, that questionnaire could be sent to either all job incumbents or a random sample of incumbents. The survey should ask respondents to rate each duty listed in terms of any or all of the following criteria:

- How *significant* it is in everyday job performance (from very significant to not significant).
- How *much time* the incumbent spends each day, week, or month on it (expressed as a percent or in time).
- How *frequently* the task is performed.
- How *difficult* the duty or task is to complete.

Once the data are compiled, look for those duties that are significant, consume a lot of time, are done frequently, and are difficult to do. The result of this step is a list of the key job duties found in the work done by most incumbents. In an early example of this procedure, Dunnette and Kirchner (1951) searched a variety of sources and ended up with a list of 35 duties found in sales jobs. Six hundred and eighty-five sales representatives from 3M rank-ordered the duties in order of importance, and the results were compiled into duty and task skills groups.

Tasks Performed

A *task* is a discrete unit of work with a definite beginning and ending. Several tasks may be involved in completing one job duty, and the same task may be followed in completing several duties. Consider an accounts payable *job* in which one *duty* is to issue payments for bills received. The *tasks* involved in completing this duty may include compiling all the paperwork into account files, double checking the accuracy of invoice statements by adding together the subtotals on a calculator, and preparing a payment authorization form. Likewise, the double-checking task may be repeated in other duties, such as balancing the books or inspecting budget reports. A *task analysis,* then, involves identifying all the key tasks done for the job duties identified. Again, the analyst may observe task performance, interview incumbents, or consult training or procedural manuals. A task list would include a list of tasks done; how each task is done; where, when, and with whom the task is done; and why it is done.

Harrison, Pietri, and Moore (1983) combined a nominal group technique approach with a critical incident procedure in working with groups of 10 or so supervisors to identify key supervisory tasks as part of a training planning process. Participants began by responding to the question: What are the major human resources problems you (the supervisor) face that prevent achieving the best results? Answers were collected in the group, then discussed and clarified. Participants then wrote the five most critical problems they faced, which were then discussed in the group to produce a common ranking of priorities. A list of supervisory tasks was teased from this information. Finally, participants were asked to recall any specific examples they had observed of these situations and what happened. This last discussion was recorded and used in developing course materials.

Identify Learned Capabilities

Developing a list of task statements is critical because the training analyst is really trying to identify the learned capabilities that are necessary to successfully execute the job tasks. This is the essence, then, of the third step:

to identify the *knowledge and skills*[2] required by the job. The procedure for identifying knowledge and skills is as much a matter of informed judgment and logical deduction as any other procedure. What the researcher is doing here is deriving and matching specific learned capabilities to task perform-ance. Continuing with the accounts payable example, several capabilities are clearly linked to task performance.

- To compile all needed paperwork, a person must *know* all the kinds of forms needed and be able to evaluate the adequacy of each.
- To double check invoice accuracy, a person must be *able to operate* a calculator, *know how to read* invoice statements and find the proper numbers, and *be skilled in* hunting down and fixing errors.

Skills are typically listed as behaviors performed or demonstrated. Consider a manager's job. One task in supervising the performance of subordinates should be setting specific performance objectives (Locke & Latham, 1990). The skill for performing this task can be defined behaviorally, such as, communicating completion deadlines and quality standards for special projects.

Schmitt and his colleagues (1993) provide a classic illustration of the entire job analysis process. In their research, they wanted to learn what capabilities were needed by clerical and secretarial personnel.[3] More than 100 secretarial personnel in the client organization were interviewed in small groups of four to six persons each. From those interviews, 174 task statements emerged, which were eventually reduced to 11 general task categories. Likewise, over 90 different kinds of KSAs (knowledge, skills, and abilities) were used in perform-ing these tasks; this long list was reduced to a shorter list of 16 KSAs. A table formed by the 11 major task categories and by the 16 primary KSAs was then used to match capabilities with tasks. The result is shown as the Task-KSA "blueprint" in Table 5.2.

Assessing Trainee Abilities

Once a list of the knowledge and skills required for task performance is established, the personnel who may be included in the training should be assessed in terms of the degree to which they possess those learned capabilities (Goldstein, 1986; Schneier, Guthrie, & Olian, 1988). One common approach lists the knowledge and skills on a survey questionnaire. Respondents then rate the extent to which a specific employee possesses those abilities, using a 5- to 9-point scale. Nowack (1991) illustrates how this procedure can work efficiently

TABLE 5.2 Blueprint for Selection Procedures Resulting From KSA-Task Linkage Judgments

Task Category	1	2	3	4	5	6	7	8	9	10	11	12	13	14	15	16
1. Maintaining and developing databases and spreadsheets, including collecting and entering information. Using databases and spreadsheets to obtain summaries and answer questions.		X[a]	X	X					X	X	X					X
2. General computer activities. Working with data files and preparing printed documents. Answers questions about computer use and printing options.		X		X				X	X	X					X	X
3. Creating and completing various company forms and ensuring that they are filed and/or distributed to appropriate personnel.		X	X	X	X		X		X	X	X					X
4. General clerical activities including answering phone, filing, handling mail, and duplicating.		X		X	X	X	X	X	X	X			X	X		X
5. Note taking, typing, and letter preparation, including editing and revising.		X		X	X	X	X	X	X	X	X	X	X	X	X	X
6. Handling travel arrangements, securing reimbursements, and completing travel expense forms.		X	X	X	X	X	X	X	X		X			X		X
7. Personnel related record keeping and handling payroll duties, including auditing and resolving discrepancies. Maintaining unit personnel files.		X		X	X	X	X	X	X		X					X
8. Coordinating office and building functions and maintaining equipment/supplies. Scheduling meetings and conferences, ensuring that necessary people and equipment arrive.		X		X	X	X	X	X	X					X		X
9. Generating reports, charts, and graphs from notes/data and ensuring their accuracy.		X	X	X	X	X	X	X	X		X					X
10. Coordinating and administering training and substituting activities.				X		X		X						X	X	X
11. Using electronic communication systems to send and receive information (file, messages, data, etc.).		X					X		X		X	X			X	X

a. X = Those KSAs for which performance of a task was considered important by expert judges, that is, mean ratings were 3.00 or above.
NOTE: The KSAs are: (1) Ability to follow oral directions, (2) Ability to read & follow manuals, (3) Ability to perform basic arithmetic operations, (4) Ability to organize, (5) Judgment/Decision making, (6) Oral communication, (7) Written communication, (8) Interpersonal skills, (9) Typing skills, (10) Knowledge of computer software, (11) Knowledge of company policies, (12) Knowledge of basic computer operations, (13) Knowledge of how to use office machines, (14) Flexibility in dealing with job demands, (15) Knowledge of communication software, (16) Ability to attend to detail.
SOURCE: From B. Schmitt, S. W. Gulliland, R. S. Landis, & D. Devine (1993). Used by permission.

EXHIBIT 5.1 Sample Needs Assessment Survey

For each of the following areas of skill, knowledge, and ability, please make two
judgments. First, rate the importance of each dimension to your current job
requirements by circling a number from 1 to 5 (1 = not at all important;
5 = very important). Second, indicate your current level of proficiency in each area
(1 = a great deal; 5 = none at all).

	Importance	*Proficiency*
	Importance of the Dimension in Performing Your Job	*Proficiency Expressed in Your Job*
Administrative and Managerial Dimensions		
Planning and organizing Ability to effectively schedule time, tasks, and activities and establish a course of action to accomplish goals.	1 2 3 4 5	1 2 3 4 5
Administrative control Ability to develop procedures to monitor and evaluate job activities and tasks on an ongoing basis.	1 2 3 4 5	1 2 3 4 5
Employee development Ability to develop the skills, knowledge, and abilities of subordinates through coaching and developmental approaches.	1 2 3 4 5	1 2 3 4 5

SOURCE: Nowack. Reprinted from *Training & Development.* Copyright April 1991, the American Society
for Training and Development. Reprinted with permission. All rights reserved.

when respondents are asked to rate both the importance of the ability (1 = not
important to 5 = very important) and that employee's proficiency with the ability
(5 = not skilled to 1 = very skilled). See Exhibit 5.1. By simply summing the
two scores for each item, a composite rating score is achieved. Note the way the
scales are calibrated: The maximum score of 10 would indicate an ability that
is very important but for which the trainee is not skilled. A simple numerical
ranking of averaged responses would make it easy to spot top priority training
needs. By averaging responses for each item on the survey, a profile of the
training needs for a group of potential trainees can be created.

Witkin (1984) recommends using a Priority Need Index (PNI) to calculate
training needs. Using a 9-point scale to rate both importance I and degree of
attainment D (or task proficiency), the PNI is calculated this way: $PNI = I \times (I - D)$.

Using the example of supervisory goal-setting, assume that the ratings given to a group of potential supervisory trainees on their proficiency in establishing performance objectives averaged out as follows: $I = 7.3$ and $D = 5$. To calculate the PNI for that item: $7.3 \times (7.3-5) = 16.79$. Similar calculations of the rated proficiencies for the other skills included in the survey would make it easy to rank and compare the relative degree of importance for training for each skill.

The survey could be sent to the job incumbents (as potential trainees) for self-rating or to others who might be familiar with the incumbent's performance, such as peers and coworkers, managers, subordinates, or even customers, regulators, consultants, or suppliers. Although the use of others complicates data collection and analysis, there is a danger in relying exclusively on self-rating. McEnery and McEnery (1987) found that individuals rating themselves tended to be more lenient and to rate their performance uniformly high (that is, they showed a halo bias). The danger from exclusive reliance on self-assessments comes in two ways: Lenient ratings mean that people think they need less training than they may in fact need, and halo errors cause a lack of discrimination in identifying the specific skills that need improvement.

There are several ways to avoid such problems. First, do not rely exclusively on self-rating, but include other rating sources. Second, where possible, use direct observations or tests of trainee performance. This could include rating employees on job performance using direct observation of their actual work or of a simulated performance, such as done through a simulation, work sample, or assessment center. For example, several years ago, I set up a performance appraisal role-play situation in which managers were videotaped conducting an appraisal discussion; the "employee" was an associate of mine trained to react to the discussion in certain ways. The videotapes were analyzed to identify typical discussion practices, both good and bad. These data were combined with the managers' self-reports on how well they thought they completed various parts of the discussion and with the results from a parallel survey form filled out by their subordinates. These multiple sources of information provided a much more detailed and precise isolation of the managers' specific training needs.

This procedure has one other use. In some cases, all potential trainees may be assessed and rated on their proficiency in each task, knowledge, and skill. Some trainees may be highly proficient in all or most categories. In these cases, it wouldn't make sense to require them to attend all or most of a training program. Trainee assessments can be used to determine whom to include *or exclude* from a training program.

Testing employees on what they know about a topic to identify current abilities and future training requirements is also possible. This approach was used with the Colorado Department of Highways to assess engineering personnel (Warrenfeltz, 1989). Program managers used certification tests developed by the National Institute for Certification in Engineering Technologies (NICET) to assess existing staff. NICET tests are knowledge tests keyed to specific engineering work tasks (such as highway construction). In this case, scores from the personnel taking the test were compared to the national average scores available from NICET. Areas of test performance below nationally based normative scores were further analyzed to identify the specific questions missed. Based on this information, a training curriculum was developed. An added benefit of this procedure was the ready acceptance of test results by the personnel taking the test, due to NICET's reputation. When information about one's current skill level is seen as valid and legitimate by the potential trainees, they are beneficially motivated to further the training process.

The results of a trainee assessment are critical to the effective planning of an HRD program. First, there are three essential descriptors of the jobs affected by the analysis: (a) the specific duties of the job, (b) the tasks associated with those duties, and (c) the knowledge and skills required to perform those tasks. All this information should be documented in a composite summary. Second, the items that could be included in a training or HRD program are listed in some relative order of need. Third, the personnel who need training—or who do not —may also be noted and factored into the plans for the training.

■ Readiness for Change Review

The front-end research assessments presented so far all seek answers to the basic question of whether training is an appropriate intervention for a performance problem. An organizational assessment shows if there is a performance problem. A performance problem analysis looks at whether instructional programming is the appropriate solution to the problem. A trainee assessment identifies what kinds of knowledge and skills should be covered by the training and which personnel should be included. Even if all of the results from these research projects point strongly toward a training intervention, training still may not be the thing to do.

A final question to consider as part of a front-end assessment involves how ready the organization is to support and adopt the changes the training should produce (Dormant, 1992). This research step has been referred to as an *organizational assessment* (Goldstein, 1986), *Stage II evaluation* (Brinkerhoff, 1991), and *analysis of the characteristics of the work setting* (Rothwell & Kazanas,

1992). Regardless of what it is called, the need for this research arises from the possibility that the trainees or the organization in which they work may resist or reject the training. So, even if training seems indicated, the practitioner should also discover what barriers might exist and how those barriers might be offset as part of a front-end assessment. Here, this research focus will be called a *readiness for change review* (Harrison, 1994).

Early in my career as a trainer, I ran headlong into an example of this problem. Around 1980, I was leading a supervisory training program for a group of managers in a large bank. One of the participants was the assistant manager in a department well known for both its morale and production problems. During the program, I covered the then-still-new process of "quality circles." About 2 weeks after the course was over, I ran into the assistant manager from the troubled department, who told me how much she liked the material on quality circles. I was immensely pleased to think that the training had succeeded, for if there was ever a place where a quality circles process would work, it was in her department. Sensing my growing need for humility, however, she quickly added that after mentioning it to her boss, he said they would do nothing of the sort. Game, set, match.

Reactions such as this have been called *resistance to change* (Goldstein, 1989) or *problems with the transfer of training*. Either way, a variety of conditions exist outside the training program that may doom even the best training. The analyst must consider these conditions as part of the front-end assessment (Yelon, 1992). Weisbord (1987) makes a case for assessing readiness for change in terms of Lewin's unfreezing model of system transformation, where diagnosis plays an instrumental role in leveraging change.

> Diagnosis no longer means unfreezing. Its function now is finding the leadership and focus likely to turn people's anxiety from impulse to fight or flee into the constructive energy and mutual support needed to transform the system. Accept that problems are everywhere, like flowers in the woods. But not everybody is ready to be helped, nor every culture amenable to remodeling. (p. 251)

In the extreme case, when there are severe and intractable obstacles in place, it may be best to avoid, cancel, or postpone the training. More practically, it may be necessary to spend time correcting or removing the obstacles before proceeding with the training. Decisions about what course of action to take will be informed by an effective readiness for change review.

How does one conduct such a review? Models and approaches to the problem go back a number of years in several fields of study. Initial concerns in this area can be traced to the "transfer of training" problem, where skills learned in a training setting do not result in transformed performance back on the job. Early attempts to identify the source of transfer problems looked at how closely the training matched the conditions of the job (Hunter, 1971; Jelsma, Van Merrienboer, & Bijlstra, 1990). This rather limited focus has been supplemented by a larger view that recognizes the effect of such noninstructional factors as the nature or degree of on-the-job task pressures, opportunities to practice learned skills back on the job, and managerial support (Brinkerhoff & Montesino, 1995). Salinger (1973) observed how a malfunctioning training process resulted from such "disincentives to training" as poor management commitment, work planning that does not include training, and production pressures that preempt training time.

Students in the fields of planned change and organization development have offered diagnoses and prescriptions for the conditions required if an organizational change is to "take." In one example, a formula for the potential for successful change (PFS) is a function of the extent to which dissatisfaction (D) with the status quo multiplied by the availability of a new model (M) for behaving multiplied by a plan (P) for the process of managing the change is greater than the costs (C) the change will require (Beer, 1980; Kolb, Osland, & Rubin, 1995). Expressed mathematically, this becomes: $PFS = f(D \times M \times P > C)$. Another example, offered by Zeira and Avedisian (1989), identified three sets of factors that significantly shape the chances of success for any planned change effort: (a) organizational factors, such as top management commitment, the presence of an evangelist for the change, and a supportive culture and structure; (b) consultant factors, which cover the extent to which the values, goals, methods, and skills of the consultant match up with the organization; and (c) environmental factors, such as the degree to which stakeholders are dissatisfied with current operations or future prospects.

Weisbord (1987), in commenting on his consulting orientation toward helping clients, advocates three critical areas for investigation: leadership commitment, good business opportunities (where returns are worth the cost), and motivation (or the degree to which people are energized to act). On the latter point, he uses a fourfold classification system for identifying employee energy levels: *contented* employees like and accept the status quo; employees in *denial* are unaware of problems and are afraid of change; *confused* employees are unsure and unfocused; and *renewal-oriented* employees are ready, albeit with some degree of unease, to move forward.

An effective review of an organization's readiness for change should address the following issues.

1. *Senior management orientation.* The manager(s) responsible for the organization in which the HRD program is targeted should be assessed in terms of the following dimensions.
    a. To what extent is the manager dissatisfied with current practices? At one extreme, the manager may be highly dissatisfied, while at the other, the manager may not be concerned.
    b. How willingly will the manager support the training process? Willingness can be demonstrated in a variety of ways, including public expressions of support, behavioral expressions of support (such as attending or participating in the training), adoption of new methods for control, factoring training into work or implementation plans, and avowed willingness to change one's own practices or style.
    c. What are the managers' expectations of any change process? To what extent will managers define the results they expect from the HRD program, and how quickly are they looking for results? Several danger signals to watch for include if the managers will not specify outcomes at all, if the outcomes they do specify are unrealistically high, or if their expectations for timing and results are unrealistically high.
    d. What are the managers' approaches to change? To what extent do they expect change to come by edict? To what extent do they understand that change will involve time, error, and developmental support?
2. *Organizational management systems.* The operational and HRM practices in place in the organization must also be examined. In some ways, this analysis parallels the performance assessment previously noted. There are three primary areas of focus:
    a. Measures of performance. What kinds of performance are measured? The classic adage in management is that you can't manage what you don't measure. If measures are not in place to gauge the performance problem areas under study, will measures be established?—and when?
    b. Compensation. Does the compensation program properly reward personnel for the performance desired?
    c. Organizational reporting. Does information about performance get to the performers in a timely manner?
3. *Performance conditions.* The conditions at the work site should be examined.
    a. Peer group/team. Is there any active interference from coworkers?
    b. Work pressures. Are the demands for current performance so great as to make it unlikely that new behaviors can be adopted?
4. *Employee orientation to change.* To what extent are employees ready to undertake the efforts and expend the energy necessary for change? Indicators of employee readiness can be seen in opinion surveys and other assessments that reveal awareness of immediate or long-term threats to organizational survival, discontent with the status quo, dissatisfaction with current practices or operations, knowledge of how competitors are providing better or different products and services, or a

general willingness to take risks, learn, and experiment. This approach is another way to use Lewin's "force field analysis" (see Harvey & Brown, 1976).

Data on these assessment issues can be collected in several ways. For senior management personnel, semistructured interviews are suggested. This could be done either individually or as a group interview. Surveys of or focus group discussions with employees often reveal how management's actions are perceived in practice (vs. the idealized version that management may offer of what it will do).[4] Organizational management systems need to be examined either by looking at policies and procedure manuals or by interviewing human resources managers. Finally, performance conditions may be assessed either through on-site observations, interviews with supervisors, or interviews with members of the work group. A survey instrument could also be used with a large group of work group members.

One final point needs to be made about this research step. An oft-stated ideal of research is that the study not disturb or alter the natural flow or progress of events. In a pure scientific approach, the researcher's presence should not change or alter the existing conditions found at the start of the study. Research should be nonreactive, according to this view. However, a readiness for change review may intentionally violate that ideal. That is, although one objective of this review is to determine whether there are barriers to change, an equally important objective is to set in motion events to remove the barriers that do exist. Thus, when interviewing senior managers, a hoped-for consequence of the discussion may be to alert the managers to their roles and to begin building their commitments to change. Research here may be used to initiate a process of change at the same time that it collects data.

■ Summary

The first research requirement facing the HRD practitioner is to determine whether training is a warranted approach for confronting a performance problem. This phase of research has been traditionally grouped under the broad term of *training needs assessment* (TNA). However, although the underlying intention of examining discrepancies between actual and preferred states is sound, there are a number of problems with the traditional approach to TNA, not the least of which is confusion over what a *need* is and how TNA research should be conducted.

A more suitable focus and direction for research is represented under the label of *front-end assessment*. Here, there are four kinds of research activities that the HRD practitioner may undertake to address the major question of whether training is the correct response to a problem. The HRD practitioner can decide whether any or all of these research projects are necessary, depending on the particular context.

An *organizational assessment* will look for shortfalls in the organization's performance. Such discrepancies may be seen in aggregate indicators of organizational performance, through benchmarking studies, from analyses of business and manpower plans, or from an audit of the human resources function. Once a performance problem is identified, the next research requirement is to locate the source of the problem: Is it caused by the larger performance system or the knowledge and skills deficiencies of the performers? This research step is a *performance problem analysis*. The practitioner should expect to find that several solutions, which may or may not involve training, are called for.

For those problems in which knowledge and skills seem to be involved, research can then discover who needs what kind of training. A *trainee assessment* starts with a job analysis, conducted in three steps: listing job duties, describing the tasks performed while doing those duties, and identifying the knowledge and skills needed to perform those tasks. Once a job analysis has been completed, prospective trainees can be studied to determine those domains in which they need training.

Finally, a front-end assessment should include an examination of the degree to which the organization is ready to support training through a *readiness for change review*. Four factors are particularly important to consider: senior management orientation, organizational management systems, performance conditions, and employee orientation to change.

Front-end assessment research focuses the practitioner on determining whether training is the right course of action to take in dealing with performance issues. Such research answers several critical planning questions. The outcome of this research should provided clear guidance for planning a solution to the problem. What this research does not do, however, is provide specific details about what the content of that solution should include. To that issue we now turn in the next chapter.

■ **Notes**

1. Rummler and Brache (1990, 1992) have developed a similar model. Performance can be analyzed at three levels: organizational, process, and job performer. At the latter level, five factors

shape performance: performance specifications, task interference, consequences, feedback, and knowledge and skills.

2. The traditional designation of learned capabilities is KSA. The K is for *knowledge* and the S is for *skills*. Psychologists tend to refer to the A as *abilities*, whereas educators refer to the A as *attitudes*. A debate over proper nomenclature is beyond the scope of this volume. Instead, I will simply refer to learned capabilities as primarily knowledge or skills required by the tasks of the job, recognizing that other learning domains, however defined, may also need to be assessed. Kraiger, Ford, and Salas (1993), in a tour de force integration, provide a comprehensive framework for identifying specific evaluation techniques for cognitive (knowledge), affective (attitudinal), and skill-based learning objectives.

3. In this study, they ultimately wanted to develop a computer-based testing procedure for selecting secretaries. Although the eventual application of this research was for selection rather than training purposes, the fundamental property of the application was the same: to assess the capabilities of job performers, albeit on a prospective rather than incumbent basis. The classic demonstration of the job analysis research process used in their study makes it a valuable example.

4. Wellins, Byham, and Wilson (1991) advocate a "readiness assessment" as part of the planning for implementing self-directed work teams. They provide a 17-item survey instrument using a 5-point Likert scale (*strongly agree* to *strongly disagree*). Factors covered by the survey include perceived management valuation of employee decision making, organizational culture and flexibility, employee interest in and skills for team work, and availability of support services (such as in the areas of human resources and information management).

6

DEVELOPING
HRD SOLUTIONS

■

This chapter reviews the application of research to the development of training solutions. In general, a *training solution* is any organized, structured program designed to teach a set of competencies necessary for successful job performance. A training solution should produce these competencies through some sort of effective learning package. An effective learning package is one that is suitable for use by those people who will be included in the training. An effective learning package, therefore, covers the specific skills needed to do a job or task well, is presented in a format and at a level that is appropriate for the people to be included in the training, and is capable of being successfully implemented. A learning package is not restricted to classroom training applications, however.

Within this context, there are four ways to apply research to the development of HRD solutions. First, the skills necessary for successful job performance must be identified. This is the process of *creating a competency profile*. Second, any characteristics of the prospective trainees that may be important to learning should be assessed. This research activity involves *identifying learner characteristics*. Two learner characteristics may be particularly important to determine: literacy and motivation. Third, it may be necessary to *customize instructional materials* for the program. Fourth, the learning package should be *pilot tested* to troubleshoot for any kinks or bugs before the program is released for use. The guidance offered in Chapter 3 still holds: It may not be necessary to research each item, depending on the circumstances. Rather, the decision to research should depend on how well and confidently the following four questions can be answered when developing an HRD solution to meet identified training needs:

- Are the specific competencies needed for successful job performance clearly identified?
- Are the capabilities and motivations of the prospective trainees known so that a learning package can be designed for their easy comprehension and use?
- Are the instructional materials properly adapted to the specific conditions, procedures, and requirements of the personnel being trained?
- Is the learning package designed effectively?

This chapter will review the research processes that can help answer each of these questions.

■ Competency Profile

A *competency* is the superior or most recommended technique for using knowledge or skills in successful job performance. As such, competencies are more than job duties, expected performance standards, or even the minimal knowledge and skills required to do a job. For example, consider the position of a customer service representative (CSR). One *duty* that may be assigned to a CSR is to handle customer product returns. The CSR may be *expected* to process returns at the point-of-sale terminal. Minimally, the CSR should *know* the policies for returns and *how to* complete the paperwork. But as anyone who has returned products also knows, there can be a world of difference in how CSRs complete the same basic transaction: One CSR can make you feel insulted, even mugged, by the time you finish, whereas another makes you want to do business with the firm again. A competency profile seeks to find out what the latter CSR did that distinguished that person's performance from that of the former. These competencies form the content and direction of the training package. That is, the training package should teach superior job competencies.

But how does one identify the essential knowledge and skills competencies for successful performance? Discovering the answer to this question is the heart of competency profile research. There are two steps involved in researching a competency profile: job analysis and the identification of competencies. Since the job analysis research protocol reviewed in Chapter 3 is reusable here, only competency identification will be discussed. Competency identification research should be built on the foundation of a strong job analysis.

An interesting example of competency profiling research was done by Rackman (1988) with regard to what he calls "large scale selling." A large sale requires multiple calls on the buyer, comes with a significant price tag and higher perceived risks for the buyer, and involves a complicated decision-making process in which the sales representative often is not present when the decision is made. Examples of large-scale sales include virtually any kind of installed system, such as computer, engineering, marketing, or human resources. At the time of Rackman's study, the traditional profile of selling skills was one in which the sales representative was supposed to control the direction of the call with chummy, rapport-building openings, forced-choice questions intended to lead the buyer to a preordained conclusion, a features and benefits-laden presentation of the product offered, quick and decisive rebuttals to "objections," and a persistent effort to "close" the sale (that is, to obtain the buyer's agreement to the sale). Skeptical about the use of these competencies in large-scale sales, Rackman and his associates accompanied business development personnel from a variety of firms to observe what they actually did when meeting with the prospects. Over 35,000 transactions were recorded; sales results served as the basis for distinguishing competent from adequate sales performance. The conclusions turned the traditional model of selling skills on its head: For large sales, highly competent sellers used the passive skills of asking the right kinds of questions and listening, rather than the active skills of presentation and persuasion. Rackman parlayed this model into a new approach to sales training.[1]

Competency Profiling

A competency profile is researched by identifying exemplary performers and then isolating what they do that is different from average performers (Rothwell & Kazanas, 1992). This can be done in several ways. For example, job incumbents or their managers could use a CIT to compile descriptions of top performance in specified performance situations; a NGT or Delphi method could be employed along these same lines. Continuing with the CSR product return example used earlier, managers, employees, coworkers, or customers could be asked to detail what a CSR did that was particularly effective or ineffective when a product was being returned. Larson and Lafasto (1989) conducted a competency profile, of sorts, on teams. They searched out a variety of teams drawn from both current and historical sources that had differing records of achievement and success. Team members were interviewed using a critical incident approach. Based on the data collected, they identified eight characteristics or competencies of high-performing teams. Boyatzis (1982) identified measures of performance as the basis for pinpointing 21 competencies of high-performing managers.

Alternatively, an experimental approach could be used in which a group of high performers could be matched (in terms of age, time on the job, location, etc.) with a group of average performers. Then, using direct observation, interviews, and so forth, a list of competencies could be derived. Regardless of how the data were collected, the analysis should look for a common pattern of practices followed by the top performers. The pattern may be detected in the kinds of behaviors used, the sequencing of those behaviors, the goals pursued, or the judgment process used to reach a decision. Once the competency list is drafted, a cross-check should find that the average or poor performers did not use these practices—at least not as much or in the same way as the superior performers. An associate of mine once looked at the differences in performance of loan collectors by studying how both the top performers and average performers went about their work. Apparently, the best collectors were able to present themselves as counselors (vs. intimidators), probed the debtor more fully, and were able to complete the conversation with a better decision about how to proceed.

Parry (1996) recommends a comparable process, which he calls a "repertory grid analysis." Job holders (either managers or employees) list at least six people whom they supervise or work with. They then differentiate those who are very competent in their work from those who aren't that good. (This activity can be facilitated by writing the names of each person on a card, then sorting the cards into two piles.) Two names are picked from the large pile, one from the smaller. The managers must now describe how the two from the same pile are similar to each other and how they differ from the third. A list of important job qualities, such as good with customers, knows products and the operating system, is created. The managers then describe the criteria for distinguishing the competent from the other performers. For example, what specifically do the competent people do that make them "good with customers"? In drafting the competencies, be sure to clarify the definition with specific behavioral examples ("Betty always smiles and makes a very personal greeting when approaching the customer and is ready to use humor and compliments to win over the customer's trust").

For tasks involving the use of knowledge and information processing, it is harder to isolate and pinpoint the competencies used, because the real work is done inside the performer's head. Still, experts in a procedure or process, such as troubleshooting a mechanical system, analyzing an accounting problem, or developing a marketing plan, follow a series of diagnostic and analytic steps that can be verbalized and drafted into a blueprint that maps the types of decisions made, the sequence by which decisions unfold, and the kinds of responses that branch from each step along the way. In effect, the mental processes of experts— also called *verbal protocols* (Bainbridge & Sanderson, 1990)—can be described through some kind of flowchart, which can in turn form the basis for training others (Zemke & Kramlinger, 1982). By discovering how a competent person thinks through a task, it is possible to train a performer how to mimic that thinking and reproduce the performance.

Rowland (1992) tape-recorded eight instructional designers (four experts, four novices) as they thought through—and out loud—how to handle a design problem. Differences in the processes described by the two groups highlighted the competencies of instructional design.

There is no single method for turning think-aloud research into mental models or verbal protocols. Valid verbal protocol information is not easy to obtain for several reasons: People may not be aware of their thinking processes, the flow of decisions may happen too quickly to note, and people may be shy or inarticulate. Given the time and effort required, think-aloud research should be used only when needed to specify the competencies of information processing and knowledge work tasks.

Bandler, Gordon, and Lebeau (1985) developed a rather elaborate method for portraying the internal thinking process followed by expert performers. Seven different elements in a thought process (such as the evaluation made of a situation, activities used, outcomes desired, and so on) should be determined, then graphed. A simpler, more accessible process includes the following steps.

1. While observing a performer doing a task, record what you see the person doing. Videotape the performance if possible.
2. Review this record with the performer, asking questions such as, "Why did you do that step? What were you trying to do? For whom or where was it intended? What were you thinking about? What did you look at or react to? What did you find out? How?" Be sure to tape-record this conversation. If possible, include several people in the review discussion. Look for decisions that must be made and operations or procedures that must be followed.
3. Construct a preliminary flow chart of the sequence of steps.
4. Verify this flowchart with SMEs. One way to do this is by giving a novice the flowchart and enough information to see whether the task can be completed

correctly. Several iterations may be required before the protocol is perfected (Bainbridge & Sanderson, 1990; Zemke & Kramlinger, 1982).

■ Identifying Learner Characteristics

This aspect of HRD research recognizes that it may be important to assess certain entry characteristics of future HRD program participants. Newstrom and Lengnick-Hall (1991) note the importance of identifying differences in individual learning styles to develop the most effective learning package through a "contingency approach" to training design.

> [Rather than] characterizing trainees as homologous adult learners who require a uniform and singular approach to training and development, [it is better to see] adult learners as a heterogeneous group requiring different approaches to training and development depending on individual differences across important charac-teristics. . . . The central assumption of the contingency model is that trainees differ between each other on many important dimensions. . . . The characteristics of a training program should be adapted to conform to the characteristics of the trainees. (p. 45)

They identify 10 possible dimensions on which to assess differences in trainee orientation (see Exhibit 6.1). For our purposes, two trainee characteristics may be particularly important to address: basic literacy and math skills, and motiva-tion to learn (Clark, 1992; Gagne, Briggs, & Wager, 1988; Holton, 1996; McCrossan & Garrett, 1992; Kazanas &Rothwell, 1994; Wlodkowski, 1988).

Literacy and Math Skills

According to a recent national survey of literacy in the United States (Kirsch, Jungeblut, Jenkins, & Kolstad, 1993), approximately half of the adult American population demonstrates literacy skills at the lowest two (of five) levels of proficiency. Given this, it would be imprudent to assume that a population of trainees will be able to proficiently read and compute materials provided in a training program, particularly if the trainee population has less of a professional or executive pedigree.

The research protocol for assessing literacy and math skills has been called a *literacy audit* (U.S. Department of Education, 1988), a *literacy task analysis* (Kutner, Sherman, Webb, & Fisher, 1991), or a *workplace educational skills analysis* (Manly et al., 1991). There are three related steps involved in a complete

EXHIBIT 6.1 Dimensions for Assessing Trainees

1. **Instrumentality:** Degree to which the trainee is concerned with the immediate applicability of the concepts and skills taught.
2. **Skepticism:** Degree to which the trainee exhibits a questioning attitude and demands logic, evidence, and examples.
3. **Resistance to change:** Degree to which the trainee fears the process of moving to the unknown or the personal effects of that process.
4. **Attention span:** Length of time the trainees can focus attention before substantial attentiveness is diminished.
5. **Expectation level:** Level of quality (process) and quantity (content) that the trainee requires from the trainer or training.
6. **Dominant needs:** Range of intrinsic and extrinsic individual needs that currently drive the trainee.
7. **Absorption level:** Pace at which the trainee expects and can accept new information.
8. **Topical interest:** Degree to which the trainee can be expected to have personal (job-relevant) interest in the topic.
9. **Self-confidence:** Degree to which the trainee independently and positively views him- or herself and thus requires high or low levels of feedback, reinforcement, and success experiences.
10. **Locus of control:** Degree to which trainee perceives that she or he can implement the training successfully back on the job with or without organizational support.

SOURCE: Newstrom & Lengnick-Hall. Reprinted from *Training & Development.* Copyright June 1991, the American Society for Training and Development. Reprinted with permission. All rights reserved.

literacy assessment: assessment of the existing literacy and math skills of trainees, analysis of the literacy and math skills required by the jobs in question, and identification of the reading comprehension level required by the materials used in the training.

Assessing Trainee Literacy Skills

The current reading or math proficiency of prospective trainees is important to determine when preparing learning packages. Depending on the size and scope of the planned training, either all future trainees or a randomly selected sample can be evaluated. There are several commercially available tests that can be used for this purpose: Tests of Adult Basic Education (TABE), Adult Basic Learning Examination (ABLE), the Wide Range Achievement Test, the Poprik-Kornegy Informal Reading Inventory, and the Laubach placement test (for lower-level abilities). TABE was the most commonly used instrument in the eight sites included in a review of selected workplace literacy programs (Kutner et al., 1991) and was the instrument of choice among most workplace literacy programs surveyed by the New York State AFL-CIO (Krusemark, 1990). Assessments may be custom-designed, too (Guglielmino, Long, & Mrowicki, n.d.). The results of the assessment should be summarized in descriptive statistics or charts, for use in developing the learning package.

Literacy and Math Job Task Analysis

Independent of the literacy proficiency levels of trainees, tasks also have a literacy or math proficiency level. As work becomes increasingly complex and information-intensive, the literacy and math requirements of jobs should increase. The planning and design of learning packages should incorporate the kinds of literacy and math tasks typically found in the tasks covered by the training. A literacy task analysis is a form of job analysis that examines the kinds of basic skills required by a job. Basic skills include reading, writing, computing, listening, problem-solving, speaking, and team building (Manly et al., 1991).

Such an analysis should begin by reviewing the duties of the job. Then, the researcher should gather information by observing competent workers, analyzing job-based documentation, and conducting interviews (U.S. Department of Education, 1988). Employees should be observed over a period of time to ensure that the researcher sees them perform all of the duties of that job. Every time the worker reads, writes, or carries out a mathematical calculation, note what that activity is, when and where it was done, and any materials (forms, equipment, and so on) that were used. Note, too, whether the activity was done individually or with others. In addition to direct observations, collect all materials that are written or read on the job. Examples of possible materials include memos, instructions, orders, bills, lists, accounting records, training manuals, job aids such as checklists, and so forth. The minimum literacy level of this material can be determined using the procedure discussed next. Finally, interview workers and supervisors to find out what skills they consider critical and important. Both Guglielmino et al. (n.d., pp. 15-17, 23-30) and Manly (1991, Appendices 7 & 8) provide detailed interview guides and observational checklists for these research activities.

Once this information is collected, it should be put into a Basic Skills Competency format. This format identifies the specific basic skills a worker must have for a given job. Core competencies can be identified. For example, core reading competencies could include reading a sign, label, chart, diagram,

EXHIBIT 6.2 Job-Related Basic Skills for a Word Processing Specialist for
                Engineering

Computing skills

   1. Calculate and plot upper and lower limits for control charts using S.O.P. from SQC
    unit and manual in order to send to manufacturing supervisors before beginning
    of shift.

Reading skills

   1. Locate the meaning, syllabication, and spelling of words using dictionary and
    thesaurus built into word processing application programs to correctly type letters
    and reports.

   2. Follow operating instructions from scanner manual, readability between 8th and
    10th grade, to program scanner, scan graphical data, and place data into appropri-
    ate file on hard drive.

Writing skills

   1. Type weekly status reports from draft materials written between the 11th and 14th
    grade level provided by supervisor in order to have ready for Wednesday morning
    staff meeting.

SOURCE: Manly, D., Mullarkey, J. E., Bentley, C., Cardona, P., Flesch, L., & Suyams, B. (1991).
Workplace educational skills analysis training guide. Madison, WI: Wisconsin Board of Vocational,
Technical and Adult Education, p. 30. Reprinted by permission.

or checklist; core writing competencies might include filling out a form or
schedule or taking notes; core math competencies could include calculating the
size of an object, counting the number of items in a bin, measuring dimensions,
or adding weights together (Guglielmino et al., n.d.). More detailed formats are
also possible. The illustration provided in Exhibit 6.2 shows, for example, the
basic skills needed for an engineering word processing specialist.

Minimum Reading Comprehension
Levels of Materials Used

The materials used in a learning package can be written and presented at
varying levels of difficulty and thereby require different minimum levels of
reading comprehension. If the required minimum reading level of training
materials is above the entry reading level of trainees, it is unlikely that there will
be sufficient comprehension, and the package will be ineffective. Assessments
of the readability of materials, although imperfect, do provide guidelines for
tailoring materials to program participants (Copley et al., 1982).

The reading level of training materials can be calculated using the Gunning Fog Index (Rothwell & Brandenburg, 1990). This procedure indicates the approximate educational grade level a reader should possess to read the material easily. Apply this procedure to the materials included in the learning package or program.

1. Select three passages from the front, middle, and end of the training *materials.* (A "passage" does not have to equal a *paragraph.*) Each passage should be at least 100 words long. Count the total number of words in each passage.
2. *Calculate* the *average* word length of each sentence. To do this, count the number of sentences in each passage. Divide the total number of words in each passage (from point 1, preceding) by the number of sentences in the passage. Select the sentence word length from the three sets of passages that best *represents* the *average* sentence length.
3. Count the number of words in each passage with three or more *syllables* (such as *syllable, represents,* or *calculate*). Do not count such words if they are proper names that are capitalized, are combinations of smaller words (such as *bookkeeper* or *handwritten*), or are formed into longer words by adding a suffix such as -es (*sentences*), -ing (*researching*), or -ed (*selected*).
4. Add together the average sentence length and the number of words with three syllables or more.
5. Multiply this sum by 0.4 to yield the minimum grade level that readers of this material should have.

Take the passage from point 1 (Select . . .) to the first sentence in point 3. There are 116 words in that passage, with 9 sentences. The average sentence length is 13 words. There are 10 words of three or more syllables (italicized in the passage). The minimum grade level for reading this passage would be 9th grade $(13 + 10) \times .4 = 9$. Materials written at a higher grade level than the typical participant has attained may not be easily comprehended.

Motivation

Motivated job-based learning (such as motivated job performance) means that learners (a) want to learn (b) about matters related to the job and (c) will persist in their learning efforts (Dweck, 1986; Mager, 1968; Wlodkowski, 1988). However, many practicing trainers are familiar with the unmotivated or resistant trainee. For any number of reasons (such as being required to attend a training program or not believing that one needs training), an adult may enter a training program with no motivation to learn—or even worse, a resistant and obstructionist motivation to any learning activities. One of my strongest memories in this regard is of a young man who was forced to attend a supervisory training program I was offering. He did not want to be there and did everything he could to communicate to me and the other trainees that he did not need to be there. The final straw was his blatantly balancing his checkbook during a review and discussion of the trainees' Myers Briggs Type Inventory results. Later, in private, I asked him to leave the class because of the disruptive effect he was having on me and the other trainees. From his research review, Holton (1996) reports, not unexpectedly, that there is a direct relationship between motivation to learn and subsequent learning.

Assessing trainee motivation may be an important first step when planning and designing learning packages. However, methods for assessing such motivation are not common. One approach looks at trainee "socialization to learning needs," which taps the expectations and orientations of trainees to a training program (Sanders & Yanouzas, 1983). An Experiential Socialization Index (see Exhibit 6.3) is administered to participants either prior to the scheduled start date or at the beginning of a program. Based on the degree of trainee acceptance of either the pivotal norms (items 1 through 9) or peripheral norms (items 10 through 18) of program participation, trainees can be classified as either *rebels* (rejecting both sets of norms), *game players* (going along with only peripheral norms), *individualists* (accepting only pivotal norms), or *motivated trainees* (accepting both sets of norms). Sanders and Yanouzas suggest involving trainees in identifying specific norms (which are then translated into items on the index) and in actively evaluating their own motivations as a basis for developing their own personal learning goals for the program.

Another approach (Keller, 1979, 1983) begins by identifying four motivational dimensions of learning: trainee interest in the content and process of instruction, trainee perception of the relevance of the goals and content of the program, trainee expectation of successfully achieving the goals and objectives of the program, and trainee experience of the actual outcomes of the program. The first three can be assessed prior to the trainee's attending the program. A simple survey questionnaire can tap into these three dimensions. Use several specific items for each dimension. For example, you could ask about trainee interest with items such as, "How interested are you in this topic (1 to 5)?" "I was very glad to discover that a program on this topic was being offered (strongly agree to strongly disagree)," "This topic is not something I think is important," and so forth. Depending on the topic and the participants, a focus group of randomly selected future trainees could also be used to obtain the same kind of information.

EXHIBIT 6.3 Experiential Socialization Index

Role of the Student in This Class

Below you are asked to indicate how much you agree with several statements describing students' behaviors, attitudes, and beliefs related to learning in classroom activities. Please respond to all items individually. Do not make ties between statements. Use the following scale for reference: strongly disagree (SD); disagree (D); mildly disagree (MD); neutral (N); mildly agree (MA); agree (A); strongly agree (SA).

As a student in this class, my role is to . . .

	SD	D	MD	N	MA	A	SA
1. Accept personal responsibility for becoming involved in learning experiences.	1	2	3	4	5	6	7
2. Be willing to participate actively in classroom analysis of learning activities.	1	2	3	4	5	6	7
3. Accept affective (feeling) learning as an important source of learning.	1	2	3	4	5	6	7
4. Recognize the importance of integrating affective (feeling) and cognitive (thinking) learning.	1	2	3	4	5	6	7
5. Be willing to engage in self-assessment.	1	2	3	4	5	6	7
6. Be willing to learn from classmates.	1	2	3	4	5	6	7
7. Be willing to make connections between classroom experiences and cognitive content.	1	2	3	4	5	6	7
8. Be willing to learn from observing my behaviors and the behaviors of others.	1	2	3	4	5	6	7
9. Believe that information learned will be useful in the future.	1	2	3	4	5	6	7
10. Accept the instructor's authority to conduct the class.	1	2	3	4	5	6	7
11. Complete assignments and readings prior to class.	1	2	3	4	5	6	7
12. Maintain a formal student/teacher relationship.	1	2	3	4	5	6	7
13. Be willing to come to class on time.	1	2	3	4	5	6	7
14. Be willing to do extra work when needed.	1	2	3	4	5	6	7
15. Accept the instructor's authority to make decisions about the relevance of course content and assignments.	1	2	3	4	5	6	7
16. Contribute to maintaining a structured classroom atmosphere.	1	2	3	4	5	6	7
17. Believe neatness on assignments is important.	1	2	3	4	5	6	7
18. Be willing to share with others personal strengths and weaknesses.	1	2	3	4	5	6	7

SOURCE: Sanders & Yanouzas. Reprinted from *Training & Development.* Copyright July 1983, the American Society for Training and Development. Reprinted with permission. All rights reserved.

There are a number of prescriptive guidelines for positively affecting trainee motivation (Keller, 1979; Keller, 1983; Mager, 1968; Wlodkowski, 1988). By assessing likely trainee motivation, steps can be taken to offset or counter potential trouble spots. These guidelines can be used prior to, during, or following a training program.

Assess Learner Disabilities?

Another potentially relevant learner characteristic to assess might be learner disabilities. Disabilities might be incidental to the learning process (such as a trainee being in a wheelchair) or could directly interfere with learning (such as hearing loss or dyslexia).

In this situation, the researcher should be aware of the legal protections covering disabled employees under the Americans with Disabilities Act (ADA). Although a detailed discussion of the ADA is beyond the scope of this book, the ADA does outlaw employment discrimination based on disability. In this context, if inadequate performance in a training program led to disciplinary action or discharge, and that performance was due to a disability covered by the ADA, there could be problems.

One solution is to make "reasonable accommodations" (such as larger type in manuals or orally administered testing) for people with disabilities. Under the law, if participants are asked to identify as part of a training program any disabilities they may have, it must be clear to all that participation in such a survey is voluntary and that any information gained will be used only for the purpose of making reasonable accommodations. Unless there is reason to suspect that some significant number of potential participants may have a relevant disability (such as, perhaps, visual or auditory perception problems among a training group composed of much older employees) or that the training will be used to make future employment decisions, an assessment of trainee disabilities should probably be avoided. Rather, the trainer should simply be alert on a case-by-case basis to learner disability issues and make appropriate accommodations whenever possible.

Summary

Assessing certain important characteristics of trainees prior to the delivery of a learning program can be very useful, because such information can help the researcher to better plan and adapt the learning package to the capabilities and intentions of the learners. Two characteristics may be particularly important:

literacy/math levels and motivation. In some cases, learner disabilities may also be important to consider. Collect information about trainees that can enable the learning package to be more effective and efficient.

Based on these research findings, the level or nature of the training program may need to be changed. In the case of literacy and math, for example, the general strategy would be to adjust the reading level of the materials to the reading level of the audience. On the other hand, if the level of reading or math proficiency required by the job is higher than the skill levels of current incumbents, a remedial basic education program may be recommended. Furthermore, it may be necessary to establish a prerequisite criterion that requires the trainee to pass a certain level of literacy and math proficiency for admission into the training.

■ Customizing Instructional Materials

Although it may be possible to use "off the shelf" training resources with a training and development program, there are important reasons for developing and using instructional materials that are as job-specific as possible. The HRD program should be given as much fidelity as possible. *Fidelity* refers to the perceived degree of overlap or similarity between what is covered in the training and the real-world, on-the-job conditions faced by the trainee. Thus, materials that refer to the specific tasks performed by the trainees on the job, incorporate current procedures and equipment, acknowledge problems or constraints on performance present in the workplace, and are taught under conditions similar to those found on the job (including noise, interference by phones or customers, work site layout, and the like) make for high fidelity in the training. There are three reasons why high fidelity is best. First, the quality of the learning in the training will be increased as trainees deal with concrete situations with which they may already have had experience. The *relevance* of the training is more apparent in this situation than in abstract or general-purpose materials. Second, by learning with materials that have high fidelity to real-world conditions, the trainees are better *prepared* for the tasks they will face back on the job. Finally, the *transfer* of training from the program back to the workplace should improve to the extent that the trainee finds identical elements in the training and on the job (National Research Council, 1991).

For these reasons, it is a good idea to increase the real-world fidelity of an HRD program as much as possible. In general, the goal of such research is to identify the significant features of actual organizational performance conditions.

Various research activities can be used to identify these features, including surveys, interviews, focus groups, reviews of secondary documentation, and observation. For example, prior to conducting supervisory leadership training, I send all participants a Case Study Worksheet on which they note any current or recent issue they faced as a supervisor. I review the returned forms to find those situations that are particularly noteworthy, significant, or difficult. I then interview the supervisor for details surrounding the case. The underlying issues are often revealed in terms of some drama, conflict, or confrontation experienced on the job. The details gathered from the interview are combined with the drama into a case study. The case study is written to disguise the location of and individuals involved in the incident, while still retaining highly specific details. From this research, I've uncovered inadequate supervisory control over employee performance, fraudulent resumes and negligent hiring, discriminatory practices toward disabled employees, and other employee problem behaviors requiring supervisory intervention (Clardy, 1994). In another program to educate managers on the issues involved in HRM (Clardy, 1996), I drew on press reports (Sears's use of incentive pay plans for auto service mechanics) to produce a case study on the ethics of compensation design, earlier needs assessment studies to produce a simulation exercise on TNA, and my own experience in benefits administration to prepare a "competition" between student groups on how to redesign a benefits plan for a midsize employer.

A prototypical research procedure in this context is the case study. A *case study* is a relatively complete presentation about a specific situation or event in the workplace. The details of the situation, such as the nature of the organization, the organizational structure, the type of work involved, and the key personnel, are provided. The drama of the event, problem, conflict, or decision is presented up to a point, after which those reading the case are challenged to analyze what has transpired to that point, and recommend future action. The basic characteristics of a case study can be reformatted into any number of other instructional formats, such as video presentations, practice exercises, simulations, games, competitions, and so forth; likewise, this material can be used for various purposes, such as role modeling, discussion, role-playing, or group decision-making.

The research procedure behind constructing a case study requires obtaining enough information to develop the case into a richly detailed story describing the *who*s, *what*s, *where*s, *when*s, and *how*s of the situation (Yin, 1989). Guidelines for developing the case include the following.

1. Specify the focus or unit of analysis. What is the case to cover: a person in a certain role (such as a supervisor), a process (such as customer service), a department or

function (such as managing human resources), the organization in general, or something else?

2. Select cases that are within the typical range of experience of most people; flashy, extremely exceptional cases may be misleading. Recently, for example, I needed to design some instructional materials for a performance appraisal refresher training course for a group of managers. In the preceding year, one manager had a very bad experience with one employee who was very disturbed. Although this situation consumed a great amount of time and energy, the specifics of the case were so exceptional that it made no sense to use that as the basis for the case materials eventually developed for the course.

3. Get important details about people and events covered by the case. For example, the age, background, personality, and organizational position of the key people involved are critical. Likewise, trace the sequence, history, or flow of events.

4. Try to obtain information about conditions or events from several different people. The more people interviewed, the more complete the picture.

5. Take thorough notes and don't be afraid to tape-record any interviews. Complete your notes as soon after the data collection procedure as possible.

6. Collect any supporting materials, such as memos, booklets, diagrams, cartoons, letters, and so forth.

7. When writing the case, put the case in the form of a story, with named characters, dialogue, and a sense of drama (Owenby, 1992).

Finally, prior to using the materials, make sure they are clear and effective. Have draft copies reviewed. To these techniques of program review we turn in the next section.

■ Program Review and Pilot Testing

Once a learning package has been developed, it should be reviewed and pilot tested before its full-scale release to "debug" it. Even though the benefits of such reviews seem obvious, it is estimated that less than 1% of educational materials are pretested (Stolovitch, 1978). There are two separate steps in this phase of HRD research: program review and pilot testing (Bachman, 1987; Piskurich, 1993).

The first research step is a *learning package review.* Three different aspects of the package may be examined: the content, the format and design, and the editorial presentation. The purpose of this review is to make sure that the package as a prototype is accurate and well structured. Although you may need several people for the review, you may also have the same person complete several different reviews.

A review of *content* should be done by a SME. The SME is given the task of making sure the information provided is accurate and adequately detailed. Since SMEs tend to consider basic training materials too simple, there is a tendency for them to cut out foundational items and elaborate on the finer points. Thus, SME reviewers should be given specific orientation and instructions for their review, including

- the learning objectives of the learning package
- the content evaluation criteria: accurate, current, not misleading, and of sufficient detail
- the need for them to make specific indications of any errors found and how they should be fixed (Piskurich, 1993)

See Exhibit 6.4 for an example of a review checklist.

A *format* review is intended to examine the structure of the learning package. Are the objectives well written? Is the material formatted in a way that is consistent and easy to use? Do all the components of the package (manual, media, etc.) link together? Other trainers or personnel involved with communications or information packaging would be best suited for this review. An *editorial* review follows closely on the heels of a content review and is designed to spot any grammatical or typographical errors. After these reviews, any obvious defects in the materials can be corrected.

The second step to this phase of the HRD research process is *pilot testing*. Unlike the review process done by carefully identified specialists, pilot testing involves a trial run of the program with real trainees in the actual training environment. A pilot test is a full dress rehearsal of the program in front of a limited but live audience (Brown & Davis, 1989). Pilot tests may be carried out on very small groups or on a single person (Brenneman, 1989). People selected to be trainees should be approximately similar in background and knowledge to the personnel who will go through the training.

In a pilot test, the trainee reviewers are given the complete learning package. The trainees go through all the exercises, activities, and instructional procedures as designed. As in the case of SMEs, trainee reviewers should be briefed on their role: to complete the package and note any problems they encounter with it. While they are going through the package, observe them to identify any problem areas. Hold a debriefing session or focus group after they have completed the program to discuss and review their reactions. For programs that teach or certify skill levels, continue the pilot testing and revision process until subjects can complete the program at the desired level of proficiency, say, 80% (Geis, 1987).

EXHIBIT 6.4 Subject Matter Review Instructions and Checklist

Instructions

Use the enclosed checklist to review the accuracy and adequacy of the content for the _____ training program. Please return your review by (date). Keep these things in mind while completing your review:

1. The intended audience for the training is _____. This audience will likely have [no] [limited] [extensive] familiarity with the subject.
2. Read the checklist before you start reviewing the training materials so that you know what we would like you to focus on in your review.
3. Review the materials. A recommended sequence is:
   a. Look at the table of contents to get an overview.
   b. Read the learning objectives. These are the specific outcomes the training is intended to produce in the trainees.
   c. Examine the materials. Look for errors, misleading or confusing statements, and so on. Please complete any assignments or exercises. Make notes directly on the materials provided where you spot problems.
4. Complete the checklist after completing the review.

Thanks for your assistance.

Checklist

Please rate the material on the categories provided by circling the number representing your most general assessment. Use this code: 1 = substantial problems, 2 = acceptable but could be improved, 3 = very acceptable with no significant problems.

1. Is the content accurate?	1	2	3
2. Is the content presented clearly?	1	2	3
3. Is enough information presented?	1	2	3
4. Is the material too complicated?	1	2	3
5. Is the information presented in the proper order and sequence?	1	2	3
6. Are the graphs, tables, charts clear?	1	2	3
7. Are the exercises and assignments appropriate?	1	2	3
8. Are all the important topics covered?	1	2	3

What does the material cover well? _____

How must the material be corrected? _____

How can the material be improved? _____

SOURCE: Derived from Piskurich, G. M. (1993). *Self-directed learning: A practical guide to design, development and implementation.* San Francisco: Jossey-Bass, p. 140.

■ Summary

There are four points at which research can bolster the development of HRD solutions to performance problems. First, research may be used to illuminate the talents that characterize superior job performance. A competency profile study serves that function. Second, the entry literacy capabilities and motivation levels of trainees can be examined. A literacy audit can reveal not only the likely entry reading and math skills of trainees but also the literacy levels demanded by the jobs and the comprehension levels required by the materials used in the learning package. Third, it may be necessary to develop customized instructional materials for use in the training. Researching situations and events to create case studies can be a valuable program development research project. Fourth, packages should be studied before being used to make sure that they are accurate in content, easy to follow in format, and free of editorial problems. A program review and pilot test should indicate any initial problems in program delivery.

■ Note

1. But not without some wear and tear. Rackman's new model of selling skills violated a long-held "paradigm" in the minds of many sales personnel about how to conduct a sales call. After making a presentation on his research at a national conference and then fielding questions from a "lynch mob of angry trainers" (Rackman & Ruff, 1991, p. 1), he found that all the overhead slides used in his presentation had been damaged and defaced. Research is not without its potential for danger and intrigue.

7

ASSESSING THE ADEQUACY OF HRD SOLUTIONS

■

The third phase of HRD research, as outlined in Chapter 1, involves assessing the adequacy of HRD solutions. There are certain basic questions facing the researcher evaluating a HRD program: How well did the HRD program work? Did the program produce change? If so, did the participants reach the desired level of proficiency (Sackett & Mullen, 1993)? These questions can be answered at two different points in an HRD program: either while the program is still operating or once the program has been completed. Evaluations done under the former condition are typically used to determine whether the program needs any modifications or enhancements; this type of evaluation is called *formative*. Evaluations of completed programs are called *summative,* because such evaluations are conducted to account for the effects of the complete program. However, *effects* can be defined in several ways, depending on the focus of the evaluation (Steecher & Davis, 1987).

Thus, rather than being a straightforward exercise in data collection and analysis, the plan for a HRD evaluation research project emerges from a series of decisions about what kind of evaluation is needed and what it should emphasize. In this chapter, the issues and techniques of formative evaluations will be reviewed first, followed by a similar examination of summative evaluations. A general framework for conducting HRD evaluation research will then be presented.

■ Formative Evaluation

For HRD programs offered several times or on an ongoing basis, it may be useful to study how well the program is being delivered "in the field" to determine whether the program needs any midcourse corrections. Formative evaluation studies collect information about a program in midflight, as it were; the data are used to make any adjustments necessary to improve further program offerings. Formative evaluations should concentrate on the performance of any critical training functions; on those aspects of the training with high visibility and importance; and on any areas where there may be indications of trainee dissent, conflict, or uncertainty (Brinkerhoff, 1991). These areas can be studied using a variety of methods and techniques.

For example, the trainer is often in the spotlight. The trainer can make a profound difference in the acceptance and acquisition of the training material. Questions about the adequacy of a trainer may be particularly salient if the person recruited to do the training has limited instructional background. In this case, direct observation of the trainer in action would be warranted. A checklist of desired and important trainer behaviors (see Exhibit 7.1) should structure the observation. The observation should be scheduled in advance so that the trainer knows the purpose of the visit, and any observation checklist should also be given to the trainer in advance. Of course, the results of the observation should be shared with the trainer to assist in any necessary improvements to the delivery and conduct of the program (Murphy, 1987).

In addition, efforts to determine how well trainees are reacting to the learning package are important. Trainee discontent or dissatisfaction can be a serious problem. If such problems do arise, the source(s) of the problems should be identified and corrections applied.

A related aspect of formative evaluation is more of an administrative activity than a research activity: reviewing the efficiency of program operations (Kaufman & Keller, 1994). This activity reviews how well resources (financial, materials, personnel, and so forth) are being used in the program. Reporting on whether the program has met budgetary parameters and delivery schedules, and on program efforts, is also necessary in this review.

In short, then, carrying out a formative evaluation should be considered whenever there is an ongoing HRD program. Begin by identifying those factors

EXHIBIT 7.1 Checklist of Trainer Behaviors

☐ Clarified learning objectives at start
☐ Was prepared for session
☐ Obtained trainee input
☐ Kept class focused on learning objectives
☐ Used media (A/V, etc.) correctly
☐ Illustrated points well
☐ Summarized key points throughout
☐ Observed time frames
☐ Facilitated group discussions well
☐ Showed interest in each individual trainee
☐ Stressed application to workplace
☐ Provided time for trainees to develop action plans

---

critical to the success of the program, which may include the trainer, participant reactions, resource usage, and any other significant aspect of the program. Collect information about the performance of those factors from observation, surveys, interviews, or reviews of relevant documents and records. Develop a summary of the findings and any recommendations for improvement. Use that information to make any changes to the program.

■ Summative Evaluation: Assessing Program Effects

Summative evaluation is the process of assessing the effects of a HRD program. Certain questions go to the heart of HRD evaluation: Did the program make a difference in learning? Did trainee performance improve after the training? Did organizational indicators of performance, such as sales, productivity, or quality, improve, decline, or stay the same? What is the value of those changes? By definition, then, an evaluation seeks to determine whether changes in some measure of performance followed the training. Furthermore, an evaluation may then render a judgment about the value of those changes.

The value of a HRD program can be expressed in one of two currencies: *merit* or *worth* (Guba & Lincoln, 1981). *Merit* is the value of a program compared to standards of training design and execution. Consider sexual harassment training for supervisors. Some programs may consist of no more than a 10-minute reading of a general policy memo, whereas others may be more involved, providing information, attitudinal self-assessments, employee survey feedback, situational case studies, and role-modeling demonstrations of how to act or not act. The relative merit of both programs can be compared against the general standards of training program design and adequacy, in which case the latter program would be more highly regarded (or meritorious) than the former. Merit is measured with a yardstick calibrated in terms of standards of learning program design and adequacy. The effects of the program are not considered.

Worth, on the other hand, is the value of the program based on the results it produces. The worth of sexual harassment training can be calculated, presumably, in terms of handling fewer complaints and less litigation, plus improved productivity from greater employee commitment and less debilitating working conditions.

A HRD program's value can be assayed, then, in terms of either its merit or its worth. Once a program is designed or operational, merit can be assessed at virtually any time. However, to assess the worth of a program's effects, the program must have run its course with time for any effects to have occurred. For example, the worth of a selection interviewing training program cannot be fully evaluated until the trainees have had time to screen and hire applicants. Evaluations that are performed on completed HRD programs to account for the results of the program are called *summative* evaluation studies (Scriven, 1973a).

Two steps are required to complete a summative evaluation: isolating the results or effects of the program and then assigning some currency of worth to those effects. Research is necessary to identify effects, whereas assigning worth is more of an issue for analysis and calculation. Research to spotlight program effects can be done in several ways and will be discussed next as models of evaluation.

Models of Evaluation Research

There are four distinctive approaches to focusing and conducting a summative evaluation. Like the blind men feeling the elephant, each approach "sees" different aspects of the HRD program, has special data requirements, and relies on unique standards for assessing program effects (Nevo, 1983). Rather than being absolutely different, however, each model is a variation on this question: What happened as a result of the training? To adequately plan an evaluation, the researcher should be aware of the choices in research direction and design offered by these models. The four approaches to evaluation, discussed more fully on the pages following, are the experimental, goals-based, stakeholder-driven, and effects-based models.

Experimental-Based Evaluation

Each HRD program is, in a sense, a hypothesis: If this training program is implemented, then certain changes (in productivity, quality, sales, employee satisfaction, or whatever) should follow. Implicitly, the accompanying hypothesis is that if the program is not used, there will be no change in the current level or trajectory of performance. Using an experimental approach, evaluation approximates classic science: Did an independent variable (here, the HRD program) cause the predicted effects in a dependent variable (learning, skills, productivity, market share, or whatever) (Rossi & Freeman, 1993)?

This approach to evaluation relies, fittingly, on the experimental method. As discussed in Chapter 1, an experimental research method has several distinctive characteristics. The nature of the changes resulting from a training treatment (experimental condition) should be hypothesized in advance of the analysis. There should be a control group used for comparison with the treatment group(s). Groups should be randomly formed. The instruments used to measure the variables under study should be valid and reliable. There should be as much control over extraneous factors as possible, and results should probably be statistically analyzed. In general, then, an experimental approach to evaluation should use as complete an experimental or quasiexperimental method as possible.

An example of an experimental approach to evaluation is Higgins's (1986) study of the effectiveness of two different kinds of stress reduction training programs. Noting that such programs are often used but seldom researched in terms of results, she administered a stress assessment before and after the training to more than 50 female participants. Participants were randomly assigned to a control group or one of two stress treatment training programs. One program taught relaxation techniques; the other taught coping skills (such as time management, assertiveness, rational beliefs). Both programs worked equally well in reducing self-reported stress, and there were no changes in the stress levels reported by the controls.

Another example of an experimental approach to training program evaluation examined the effects of a sales training program at R. H. Donnelley and Sons (Montebello & Haga, 1994). To compare the costs to the benefits of the week-long training program, researchers first looked at the number of sales closed by a group of trainees after the training. Although the results seemed impressive, it was impossible to tell to what extent the results could be attributed to the training. So, they created, after the fact, a control group of other sales representatives in the firm who had not gone through the training, matched to the trainees in terms of years of experience on the job. When the sales performance of the two groups *prior* to the training was compared, the untrained group earned slightly (but statistically insignificantly) more than the group to be trained. However, an analysis of the real gains in sales performance between the two groups *after* the training revealed a substantial and significant improvement for the trained group over the control group. This evaluation provided strong evidence that the training produced instrumental effects on sales performance. In this case, the worth of these changes was relatively easy to identify.

Goal-Based Evaluation

This model assumes that goals and objectives for the HRD program have been established at the outset and were used to guide the development and delivery of the HRD program.[1] These goals and objectives are then used as the baseline against which to evaluate the effects of the program. Were the goals and objectives met? If so, to what degree (Scriven, 1973a; Tyler, 1942)?

The basic procedure for carrying out this kind of evaluation is as follows.

1. Operationalize the goals and objectives into measurable indicators of performance. Program goals might include such organizational outcomes as reduced turnover (for supervisory training) or improved sales (for sales training). Learning objectives set for the program could also be assessed.

2. Collect information about performance on these indicators. At a minimum, information should be collected about the degree to which each program goal or objective was met *after* the program was completed.

3. Analyze how well the program goals were achieved. For example, did all participants answer at least 90% of questions on a final test correctly? Did the sales of new product X rise by 10%? Also important may be to establish that performance in the areas covered by the goals (learning, productivity, sales, etc.) did in fact improve as a result of the training. There would be little use in showing that all of the goals of the program were met *after* the program if the goals were already being met *prior* to the program.

Stakeholder-Driven Evaluation

For any program, there will be various stakeholder groups with an interest in the nature, direction, and outcome of the training. Stakeholders may include executive decision makers, program managers, trainers, trainees, and others (such as the customers, either paying or internal, of the people being trained). Each group will have its own concerns about the program and will need different information about the program. A stakeholder-driven evaluation locates stakeholders to discover their interests and information needs. The evaluation then determines the effects of the training in terms of those interests and concerns. In effect, each stakeholder's interest becomes the spotlight used to illuminate selected aspects of the HRD program's performance (Guba & Lincoln, 1981; Patton, 1980; Stufflebeam et al., 1971).

Executive management with decision-making authority over program use, funding, and support is a particularly important stakeholder group. To make appropriate decisions about HRD program, decision makers often need information that answers questions such as: How well was the HRD program planned? Were the goals of the program appropriate? How well was the program actually conducted? What actually happened as a result?

Stakeholder-driven evaluation begins by identifying program stakeholders and their needs for information about the program. Once those needs are specified, evaluative standards or criteria for judging the quality of results should be negotiated and the plan of evaluation finalized. After the data are collected and analyzed, the information must be presented in such a way as to address the stakeholders' questions.

An assessment of a police training academy curriculum illustrates a stakeholder-driven evaluation (Talley, 1986). The Oakland, Michigan, police training program had apparently evolved over the years without rigorous planning or analysis, and criticisms of the training had been growing. Decision makers needed information about the adequacy of the curriculum to respond to the criticisms and make any needed adjustments. A sample of 27 Oakland officers, recent academy graduates with 1 to 3 years of experience, were asked to identify core police tasks from a comprehensive list of police duties assembled from a statewide job analysis. Over 300 tasks were selected as essential. Respondents also noted whether they performed the task and, if so, how well the academy training had prepared them for the task. A 5-point Likert scale (1 = *totally inadequate,* 3 = *satisfactory,* 5 = *excellent*) was used to rate the perceived adequacy of the training for each task. Respondents were also asked to identify three tasks for which training needed the most improvement. Answers were totaled and ranked. Average scores of 3 or less for any item signaled a curriculum deficiency. Based on the results, program shortcomings were identified.

Effects-Based Approach

An HRD program may have any number of effects, some good (such as learning needed skills or networking with other people in an organization who face similar performance issues) and some bad (such as demotivation). The effects may show up firsthand in the trainees, indirectly in others affected by the trainees (other employees or customers), or in various organizational outcomes (such as productivity, sales, service, etc.). However, these effects cannot always be predicted. An effects-based approach to evaluation looks for the effects of an HRD program and then attaches some value to those effects (Scriven, 1973a, 1973b).

This approach is different from the goals-based approach in that the effects-based approach begins by *intentionally ignoring* the professed goals of the HRD program. For this reason, this approach to evaluation is called *goal free* (Scriven, 1973b). The rationale for this position is that by learning what the goals of the program are up front, the evaluator becomes biased and will likely miss other, unintended effects. Rather than focusing exclusively on defined performance outcomes, the goal-free evaluator casts a broad net to capture all the effects, good or bad, of the program.

In practice, then, an effects-based evaluator would avoid learning about program goals in favor of identifying all the possible people and performances that could have been affected by the training. This means conducting unstructured interviews with not only program participants, but also their bosses, coworkers, and others, to determine how they were affected by the program.

■ HRD Program Evaluation: An Integrated Approach

The existence of different models of HRD program evaluation indicates that evaluation research can proceed in a variety of directions, while ostensibly still involving evaluation. In some cases, the researcher may need to conduct one of these approaches exclusively. If, for example, there is a general question about a program (such as, Did the training make the difference in performance as hypothesized?), then a single-focused evaluation plan (here, an experimental one) is indicated. However, the HRD research practitioner can still wonder, given the variety of approaches available to conducting an evaluation, if an integrated, all-weather approach to HRD program evaluation is possible. The answer to that question is *yes,* and a general approach to program evaluation is outlined in Table 7.1, with a fuller discussion of each element following. Note that the actual shape and dimensions of the evaluation depend, in part, on how certain questions posed in the planning stages are answered. Thus, even under

TABLE 7.1 General Approach to HRD Program Evaluation

I. Establish the scope and focus of the evaluation.
   A. Model the program.
   B. Identify key stakeholders and determine what specific issues, if any, they want addressed by the evaluation.
   C. Identify and assess planned program outcomes.
   D. Negotiate what the evaluation plan will cover with any decision makers.
   E. Plan the evaluation research project.
II. Document the program.
   A. Describe the program.
   B. Assess program implementation.
III. Collect information about program outcomes.
IV. Analyze results.
V. Write and communicate the report.

this general approach to evaluation, the final research design is contingent on certain planning decisions.

Establish the Scope and Focus of the Evaluation

There are five steps to the initial planning activities of a HRD program evaluation study.

Model the HRD Program's Effect

Evaluation planning should begin with a model of the chain of actions and expected results that describes how the program is assumed to work. A program model is a picture of the causal chain or production function that presumably transforms inputs into certain defined outputs. The logic behind a program model starts with the assumption that a HRD program is designed and offered with the goal of teaching new abilities. New abilities should lead to improved job performance; better job performance should lead, in turn, to improvements in desirable organizational outcomes, such as service, profitability, or market share (Brinkerhoff, 1991; McDonald, 1987). A program model is shown as an open system, in which training is taken as an integrated system of goals, inputs (training materials and trainees), training activities, and training effects, such as

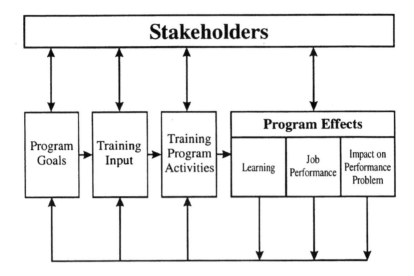

Figure 7.1. Modeling the HRD Process

learning results, employee job performance, and organizational outcomes. In addition, as explored more fully on the following pages, there are stakeholders (decision makers, managers, participants, clients and customers, and others) whose interests span the breadth of the HRD program. The generic open-systems model for HRD programs is shown in Figure 7.1.

In general, then, planning for an evaluation study should start by filling in the blanks under each variable in this model to orient the researcher to the program. In particular, at this point, the researcher should concentrate on identifying likely or expected effects of the training. Finer detail on all parts of this model will be acquired in the course of the actual evaluation research.

There are several reasons to sketch a model of the HRD program. As noted, the model orients the researcher. The model provides a checklist of factors the evaluation should look at. The model shows the rationale for linking HRD program activities and outcomes. A good model should aid in negotiating the evaluation plan. Finally, and perhaps of most importance, the model indicates the kinds of effects expected from the training. The snowballing or cascading effects of the program, from learning to behavior changes to organizational performance, can be projected and estimated.

Identify Key Stakeholders
and Their Information Needs

Program evaluation occupies a motherhood and apple-pie position in the world of HRD: It is one of those things that everyone says is great. However, completing a full-scale program evaluation of the kind proposed here is frequently left to the discretion of HRD program managers and is often not done. To say that program evaluation is discretionary for HRD managers is also to say that stakeholders often do not look for or depend on the results of the evaluation. Many trainers find that when evaluations are done, they are often done without the awareness, backing, or expectation of important stakeholders. Yet this is not an excuse to avoid program evaluation: Good evaluations should be a regular and important step in all HRD work. Thus, even though stakeholders *can* often be circumvented in HRD evaluation, that does not suggest that they *should* be.

Another critical first step in carrying out an HRD evaluation, then, should be to identify key stakeholders to find out what kind of information they need or would like to have about the program. Certainly, one stakeholder group to include at this step is the group of key decision makers. Other groups may also be contacted. These groups should be given the opportunity to define what issues and questions they would like addressed in the evaluation. These information needs become the foundation for planning the evaluation. Sometimes stakeholder groups cannot articulate any specific agenda for evaluating the program. If that is the case, then the evaluator should revert to an evaluation that looks at goal achievement, with an open eye to any other effects (positive or negative) the program may have produced.

Identify and Assess Planned Program Outcomes

Regardless of stakeholder interests and concerns, an evaluation should examine the extent to which the intended outcomes of the program were achieved. However, as noted, effects can take various forms and exist at differing levels of direct connection to training. For HRD program evaluation purposes, there are three main classes of effects that can be studied (Kirkpatrick, 1987; Spencer, 1986).[2]

Participant Learning. What have participants learned as a result of the HRD program? Although learning does not guarantee eventual performance improvement, it is a direct and expected outcome of the program. Indeed, as Kraiger, Ford, & Salas (1993) contend, "the most fundamental issue of evaluation is whether trainees have learned the material covered in training" (p. 311). Training *evaluation,* to these authors, concerns the degree of change seen in the domains of learning; studies of training *effectiveness* concentrate on changes to organizational conditions that should follow from training.

In general, learning can occur in the cognitive, affective, and skill capacities of trainees; that is, in what people know, how they feel about things, and in their behavioral skills in performing tasks (Kraiger, Ford, & Salas, 1993). Moreover, different kinds of learning may happen in each domain. For example, there are at least three kinds of cognitive learning outcomes possible: declarative knowledge of facts and procedures (assessed early in training using traditional tests of information recall), the organization of knowledge (assessed by comparing the trainee's map, mental model, or cognitive structures of a field of knowledge against a master's map), and cognitive strategies for solving problems. Skills-based learning can be assessed in terms of how correctly steps are performed or the degree to which steps are performed automatically (even given some degree of task interference). Finally, training may be designed to produce changes in attitudes about a subject (such as more commitment to organizational goals and directions) or in motivation. Evaluation practices must be matched to the kind of learning expected from the training.

Another issue specific to learning evaluation centers on the need for and use of comparison data. To judge whether learning took place, the evaluator must have information about the participants' levels of knowledge before and after the training. The best recommendation is to test participants before the program begins and after the program has been completed.[3] In an interesting twist on this approach, Haccoun and Hamtiaux (1994) used a testing procedure that included a set of test items about material *not* covered by the training. Reasoning that correct training-based test scores should increase, whereas correct nontraining-based scores should remain unchanged, they administered a multiple-choice test to the training group and a control group both before and after a management training program. Two parallel test forms were used, containing 26 relevant and 11 irrelevant items. Test scores performed as predicted, with the only score improvements occurring on the training-relevant items for the training group; all other scores in the pre- and posttraining comparisons—for the control group and for the nontraining items for both groups—remained low and stable. These findings lend even more credence to the learning effects of training programs.

Another common approach to learning evaluation uses self-report measures of learning. Rather than directly testing learning achievement directly, respondents rate how much they think they've learned. For example, participants might be asked to rate how much they know about some subject (such as writing performance evaluations or making prospect calls) using a 10-point scale (where 1 = *almost nothing* to 10 = *high expertise*). Self-report assessments can be given out before and after a training program; differences between scores are taken as evidence of learning produced by the training. These kinds of measures are widely used because they are easy to develop and convenient to administer. Unfortunately, as usually administered, self-report measures often *under*estimate the learning that has taken place, because participants often *over*rate what they think they know in the pretest (Mezoff, 1981). To correct for this inflated entry opinion, participants can be given *two* self-reports to complete at the conclusion of the training. The first is the standard form on which participants rate how much they know about the subjects now (POSTtraining). Participants are then given a duplicate form but asked to think back to how much they knew about the subject at the start of the program, rating how much they knew about the subjects THEN. This method is called a POST-THEN approach to self-report assessment. This approach provides a truer picture of the amount of learning program participants believe they have acquired.

Learning can also be evaluated in other ways. For example, civilian graduates of a Navy personnel management program were evaluated on their learning 3 to 6 months after completing the program. The assessment procedure used a series of "real life" case studies reflecting the topics included in the training; a checklist of the training competencies that should be used in the cases was prepared. The ex-trainees were asked how they would handle each situation, and if the trainee "used" a competency in handling the case situation, it was checked. If the trainee mentioned using the competency again in related cases, the competency was considered learned (Erickson, 1990).

Behavior Transfer to the Job. Learning is one thing; using what was learned when back on the job is another. Did the trainees act differently on the job, presumably as a result of what was learned?[4] Who is using the training? Did the training work for some and not others? Which parts of the training are being used? How often is the training being used? How well is it being used?

There are several ways to assess the degree of transfer. Respondent self-reports of changes in workplace performance are one option. For example, participants could be asked: "Have you used procedure X on the job, and if so, how often?" Another option that can be used alone or in combination with self-reports is a survey asking for coworkers', managers', subordinates', and others' perceptions of the participants' performance. Recent initiatives in peer review or 360 feedback are the basic platform for using this form of assessment (London & Beatty, 1993). A third alternative relies on the use of trainee action plans (Salinger, 1979). Trainees complete an action plan at the end of the program. The plan lists the things the participant wishes to do back on the job as a result of the training. The trainer keeps a copy of the plan. Three to six months later, the participant is interviewed about what actions have been taken, using the action plan as a prompt. The results can be analyzed in several ways: by calculating the percent of actions actually taken (vs. the number listed), the relation of the action items to course objectives, or the reasons for not trying or failing to carry out the action plan. Where possible, verify this information by checking with coworkers.

A fourth approach to evaluating behavior transfer is through a "levels of use" framework used to gauge the extent to which an innovation has been adopted. Hall and his associates (1975) catalogued eight progressively more inclusive and elaborate levels of use, ranging from nonuse through orientation and preparation to mechanical (rote) use, routine use, and then to refinements in use, integration into broader practice, and finally renewal (critical assessment and search for alternatives). Nielsen and Turner (1985) used this framework to examine the extent to which teachers transferred back to their classroom the training they received in three new curricular programs. Using a structured interview guide, interviewers contacted the teacher-trainees and were able to determine different levels of applied usage among the three programs.

Effects on Organizational Performance. Just as the general sequence of front-end assessments descends from broad, organizational measures down to more specific individual assessments, so do HRD evaluations retrace the process back from individual assessments of learning and behavior change up to organizational performance. Of course, the organizational effects examined in the evaluation should be the ones first detected as potential sources of problems. These are the outcomes that triggered the HRD program to begin with; these are the same outcomes the HRD program should be expected to favorably affect.

The main issue here is one of analysis: separating out the true effects of the program from the secular forces that may also be in play. Consider a customer relations training program intended to improve the company's customer perceptions of service quality. If customer ratings go down, does that mean that the training was counterproductive, if staff cutbacks and "get tough" service management standards were instituted in the same period? If customer ratings go up, does that mean the training was successful, if substantial price reductions were made at the same time? Methods for addressing this issue in the research design are discussed in a later section.

Negotiate the Nature of the Evaluation Plan

If decision makers or other stakeholders are closely interested in the evaluation, it will be important to agree with them about the course and nature of the evaluation. The more active the stakeholders, the greater the need for an agreed-on evaluation plan. There are two primary forces at play in HRD evaluation research that require a negotiated agreement on the evaluation plan. First, as noted, there is no simple "one size fits all" model of HRD evaluation; different approaches to evaluation lead to different kinds of assessments. Without clear agreement, an evaluation may easily go in the wrong direction, waste time and resources, and not provide relevant, needed information. Second, evaluations can be highly political. Different stakeholder groups may be affected by programs in different ways, and evaluations can threaten or be seen as a tool of those interests. In the process of negotiating a plan, the information needs and interests of different stakeholder groups should be assessed where feasible and included in the data collection process (Popham, 1975; Steecher & Davis, 1987). A HRD program evaluation must rely on a research plan customized to fit program circumstances and stakeholder needs. The researcher must negotiate and agree to an appropriate evaluation design with the party receiving the evaluation. Different stakeholder groups may require different negotiations.

There are several critical issues to consider during the negotiations. First, what do the stakeholders need to find out about the program, and how will they use that information? There should be agreement about what questions the evaluation should answer. Second, what standards will be used in judging the value of the effects? Should value be presented in financial terms? Third, the general scope, structure, and operation of the evaluation should be understood. Fourth, as needed, the costs of the evaluation should be estimated and a commitment obtained about providing sufficient resources to meet those costs.

Plan the Evaluation Research Project

Like other HRD research activities, an evaluation research project should be carefully planned in advance. The plan should stipulate the specific timing, information collection procedures, coverages, and costs for completing the evaluation (Worthen, 1977). The agreed-on plan should be committed to writing,

TABLE 7.2 Outline for Evaluation Research Plan

Program: _____

   I. Program description:
      a. Target population covered by the program
      b. Intended effects on participants and the organization
      c. Program operations and activities
         • trainers, instructors, staff
         • duration
         • content covered
         • schedule of learning activities
      d. Offerings: schedule and locations
      e. Any unusual events during delivery

  II. Stakeholders and their priorities for the evaluation:

 III. Evaluation procedure:

Step	Data gathering activity	Type of data to collect
1		
2		
3		

 IV. Analysis procedures

  V. Schedule and cost

with each party receiving a copy. Table 7.2 offers a template for a model evaluation plan.

Document the Program

Describe the Program

Once the research plan is done, the initial data gathering can begin with a thorough description of the HRD program itself. The thing being evaluated—that is, the HRD program—must be fully described. This aspect of the evaluation should produce rich detail about the following:

- *Program goals,* as listed in planning documents or from interviews with training designers, decision makers, and so forth
- *Program administration,* including such matters as announcements of the program, manager involvement (pro, con, or neutral), notification of participants, program pricing or costs, location(s), and staff support
- *Participants,* a list of the personnel included, how they were selected, attendance levels, and so forth
- *Program activities,* as shown in program schedules or manuals, as recalled by participants, or as directly observed. Any program tests or assessments that were conducted should be noted. Where appropriate, details about the validity and reliability of learning activities, assessments, and so forth should also be reported
- *Program implementation,* so that in the case of programs offered more than once, at different sites, or with different groups, descriptions of any variations in program implementation are noted. For example, were there any unusual events surrounding or affecting the training? [5]

Assess Program Implementation

An assumption often made in evaluation studies is that the treatment being assessed (here, an HRD program) was delivered in a uniformly consistent manner. For programs that are offered on several occasions, to different groups or at different locations, this assumption is questionable (King et al., 1987; Mark, 1983). As any trainer in this situation knows, program delivery can vary because of trainer fatigue or boredom or because of unique participant group characteristics (see Footnote 4). If training is offered repeatedly, it can be worthwhile to check on how consistently it is delivered. There are two aspects of an HRD program's implementation that should be assessed: context (such as location or setting, participants, interruptions, and so forth) and activities (or the degree to which the program was carried out as planned). The researcher can fashion ways to assess the implementation using observations, interviews, or checklists. For example, either the trainer or the participants in a program could complete a checklist indicating whether a series of items were covered in the training or to provide an estimate of how much time was spent on each item (Scheirer & Rezmovic, 1983).[6]

Collect Information About Program Outcomes

The steps and procedures to follow in an evaluation project are fundamentally a function of the kind of expected outcomes, goals, or stakeholder interests driving the HRD program. Sufficient information should be collected on those items to permit a judgment about the extent to which planned results occurred.

One important data collection issue is how to bring the most credibility to the results of the study. A general operating principle in this regard is *triangulation* (Greene & McClintock, 1985). Rather than relying on only one indicator of program effects, we are cautioned by the triangulation principle to use several different and independent kinds of data, observers, and methods to collect information. If the data from different sources all point in the same direction (or triangulate on a conclusion), one can be more confident in the assessments made of program effects. Greene and McClintock (1985) used a "mixed-method" triangulation design to evaluate an adult education program. Participants completed a questionnaire about the program and nonparticipating stakeholders were interviewed to discover their opinions of the program's effects. Different sources of information were approached with different methods, creating two independent sets of data about the same HRD event. On some items, the different methods found similar results, strengthening the conclusions.

Analyze Results

The general purpose of an HRD program evaluation is to attach value to the effects produced by the program. For that reason, it is critical that the evaluation design clearly identify what the effects of the HRD program are; in turn, this means being able to rule out alternative explanations of why those effects may have occurred. This is essentially the same set of concerns discussed in Chapter 1 as threats to validity. As you may recall from an example there, the effects of increased sales were observed after the simultaneous introduction of both a training program and a rich incentive plan. Were the results due to the training, the incentive plan, or both? The analysis should consider whether there are any other ways to explain the results, other than as the effects of the HRD program. Obviously, to be confident about one's assessments, these competing explanations must be examined to take them into account or to rule them out (Brinkerhoff, 1991; Rossi & Freeman, 1993). The following are all possible competing explanations for program results.

- *Spontaneous improvement.* Improvements in performance may have simply occurred because the trainees obtained more on-the-job experience or were driven to improve more than the control group. Consider a group of trainees attending a selling skills training program soon after becoming sales representatives. Their sales may have improved simply as a result of a natural rise in their skills from making repeated sales calls in the regular course of doing their job. That is, their performance might have improved even without the training. The check on this factor would be if improvements occurred for many personnel regardless of how long they had been on the job. Similarly, consider a group of sales trainees who volunteer for the training: This group could be so highly motivated to perform better that, again, performance improvements would have occurred even without the training. The check here would be if there were overall gains regardless of the degree of trainee motivation.

- *Interfering events.* Were there any special events that happened during the course of the HRD program or its aftermath that may have caused the results? Are the effects found only in the trainee group and not across the board? Staying with the sales training example, improvements could have been the result of a particularly forceful motivational speaker who made a presentation to the sales force around the time of the training. In this case, one would expect this tide to lift the sales performance of all sales representatives, not just trainees. Conversely, product price increases might dampen sales, even though training participants came out of the training effectively using the skills they learned. Here, everyone's sales should ebb.

- *Trainee rating error.* Like other raters, trainees may be guilty of halo or severity errors when they evaluate their training (Newstrom, 1987). This would be particularly likely with self-report assessments. For example, strong personal reactions to a trainer may tint participant assessments of all aspects of the program. Thus, a trainee who strongly identified with the trainer would be expected to rate all aspects of the program (presentation, objectives, activities, learning, etc.) highly; the obverse would be expected from a trainee who strongly disliked the trainer. Ratings would be shaded similarly across all factors; uniformly very high or very low ratings could be evidence of halo/severity error. Triangulation is a helpful preventative to this problem (Newstrom, 1987).

Sackett and Mullen (1993) note that a number of threats to validity may be assessed relatively easily. For example, participants could be asked whether other events happened that they reacted to during the course of the HRD program. For short, 1- or 2-day training programs, many alternative explanations may be logically ruled out.

Cost-Return Analysis

The ultimate analysis for judging program worth is some form of cost-return analysis (Cascio, 1982; Kearsley, 1982). Such analyses calculate the worth of a HRD program in monetary terms, with program costs serving as the common denominator. Four categories can be used to classify program costs: direct program expenses, administrative overhead, general organizational costs, and participant expenses. Various kinds of effects or benefits can then be calculated.

In this context, there are two principal forms of HRD evaluation. A cost-*effectiveness* analysis puts HRD program effects into some common metric, such as the percent of learning objectives successfully achieved. For example, at Florida State University, a large lecture course in geology was converted into a self-instructional system. To evaluate the relative learning effectiveness of this program, two other learning packages (a small-group instructional model and a commercially developed instructional package) were also tested. When the costs of each program were compared to the learning results obtained, the best solution was the commercially developed package (Doughty & Stakenas, 1973).

A cost-*benefits* analysis puts program effects into financial terms. Pine and Tingley (1993) calculated the financial benefits from a 2-day team-building program they provided to intact teams of maintenance workers at a jet engine manufacturing facility. Using a design that included control groups, they looked at differences in response and completion time for equipment maintenance tasks before and after the program. Total time differences were then converted into dollars. Comparing the estimated financial savings in time to the costs of the program, they judged the team-building program to have been most cost-beneficial. There are also more traditional forms of financial analysis, such as a program's payback period, its internal rate of return, and its return on investment (Basarab, 1990).[7]

Write and Communicate the Evaluation Report

A written report is essential for concluding the evaluation project. The report should be easy to use. This means that conclusions, answers to any specific questions, and recommendations should be clear and specific. In general, the following format outlines how an evaluation report should be presented.

1. *Executive summary.* In one or two pages, summarize the report. In brief paragraphs, capsulize the report's content (that is, summarize all the sections listed in the following points). Use bulleted items to highlight lists and other key points.

2. *Introduction and overview.* In this section, describe the HRD program. Provide a history of the program. Present the model of the program. Identify program goals and intended outcomes.

3. *Evaluation research method.* Here, describe the evaluation procedure itself. Describe the evaluation approach used and why it was selected. Indicate how the evaluation was commissioned and the stakeholder audience(s) to which it is addressed. Note any specific questions posed to the evaluation process. Describe how and from whom information was collected. Present any needed information

about the data collection instruments (copies of interview guides, observation checklists, etc. should be included in an appendix). Indicate how the data were analyzed. Note any limitations and caveats for interpreting the research.

4. *Presentation of findings.* In this section, provide the data. This would usually include tables or charts summarizing the information in addition to analytic calculations. For example, calculations of the program costs or dollar returns should be shown, along with any cost-return calculations.

5. *Conclusions and recommendations.* Finally, present your conclusions. What do the data tell you about what happened? List your recommendations and the rationales for each.

When there are stakeholders, the report should be reviewed with the group.

■ Summary

HRD program evaluation is similar to the weather: It is always mentioned, but not much is done about it. An evaluation should identify what effects the program developed and assign some value to those effects. HRD program effects may be determined using one of several different kinds of research models: experimental, goals-based, stakeholder driven, or effects-based.

These four approaches may be integrated in a general, five-step strategy of program evaluation. Step one defines the scope and function of the evaluation by sketching out a model of how the program should function and by identifying key stakeholders. Program outcomes should be identified in terms of the learning, level of transfer to the job, and organizational results that should be obtained. An evaluation plan, agreeable to the stakeholders, should be prepared. Step two documents the program's operation and implementation. Information about program outcomes is collected in step three, leading to the analysis of results in step four. Various forms of cost-return analysis can be completed to further establish the worth of a program. Finally, a report summarizing the research project, findings, and recommendations should follow.

■ Notes

1. Mager (1972) proposed a goal analysis method for translating desired results into concrete programmatic outcomes. For the purpose of this review, it is assumed that goals, however established, do exist and are available for use in the evaluation. On the other hand, a HRD program without clear goals up front may not be capable of being assessed using this model.

Yet another consideration is evaluating the merit of program goals themselves. Are the goals of the program good and appropriate ones? Are they important? Sophisticated training programs with secondary or trivial goals are ultimately trivial, not sophisticated.

2. The classic statement about the types of HRD outcomes, put forward by Kirkpatrick in 1959 (but see Kirkpatrick, 1987), included a fourth type of outcome called *participant reactions,* how participants feel about the program: Did they like it or not? In the training world, this form of evaluation is sometimes referred to as a *happiness sheet.* There are certain basic guidelines for assessing this kind of evaluation, such as asking about important aspects of the program, asking about expected use and value of skills learned in the program, and using easy-to-complete worksheets (Spencer, 1986).

Brinkerhoff and Gill (1994, see pp. 51-52) contend that relying on reaction measures deflects attention from the more important issues of how much learning and transfer occur from the training. Furthermore, as Holton (1996) notes, there is little correlation between participant reactions and the amount of participant learning.

Collecting participant reactions to a program is not totally without value, however. One potentially useful application of participant reaction data is in the formative evaluation process. By learning how participants react to and feel about the training, possible faults in program delivery may be exposed for correction.

Otherwise, participant reactions say little about the effects of training on the outcomes that are likely to be most critical: learning, on-the-job behavior change, and organizational results. Too often, this is the only form of evaluation conducted, and no further investigations of program effects are pursued. For these reasons, participant reactions are not valuable to summative evaluation studies and should be relegated to a secondary status.

3. There can be collateral benefits to the learning process from preprogram learning achievement testing (Mezoff, 1983). Pretesting can help improve learner motivation by pinpointing knowledge and skills deficiencies and can be a source of learning in itself. Pretesting can act as an "advance organizer," alerting the trainees to upcoming topics and concepts. A pretest keeps the trainer focused on the key points of the program, and it signals a degree of seriousness about the training by noting participant progress on those items.

4. Holton (1996), in his recent criticism of Kirkpatrick's (1987) classic model of evaluation, suggested that the behavioral transfer variable be referred to as *individual performance.* According to Holton, the two direct outcomes of any HRD programs are learning and individual performance. The term *behavior transfer* will be used here to retain connections with the transfer of training literature.

5. I once heard a trainer describe his experience training a group of civil service employees in the New York City area. Apparently, this group was particularly disruptive and difficult, prompting him to expel several people from the program. One of the expelled trainees was an attorney who, according to the trainer, could not complete one sentence without using the "F word" in an eloquent yet argumentative response to most any point the trainer tried to make. The program continued downhill from there. When evaluating a program, it is very helpful to know about any such incidents.

6. See King et al.'s (1987) appendix for a detailed set of questions for evaluating program implementation.

7. The mechanics of cost-effectiveness and cost-benefits analysis are involved and beyond the scope of this book. Interested readers should consult competent texts in this field, including Cascio (1982), Kearsley (1982), Schonberg (1993), Spencer (1986), and Swanson and Gradous (1988).

REFERENCES

Andersson, B. E., & Nilsson, S. G. (1964). Studies in the reliability and validity of the critical incident technique. *Journal of Applied Psychology, 48*(6), 398-403.

Arens, A. A., & Loebbecke, J. K. (1984). *Auditing: An integrated approach.* Englewood Cliffs, NJ: Prentice Hall.

Atwood, H. M., & Ellis, J. (1971). The concept of need: An analysis for adult education. *Adult Leadership, 19*(7), 210-212, 244.

Bachman, L. L. (1987). Pilot your program for success. *Training & Development, 41*(5), 96-97.

Bainbridge, L., & Sanderson, P. (1990). Verbal protocol analysis. In J. R. Wilson & E. N. Corlett (Eds.), *Evaluation of human work, a practical ergonomics methodology* (pp. 169-201). London: Taylor and Francis.

Bales, R. F. (1951). *Interaction process analysis.* Reading, MA: Addison-Wesley.

Bandler, L. C., Gordon, D., & Lebeau, M. (1985). *The emprint method: A guide to reproducing competence.* San Rafael, CA: FuturePace.

Bartlett, C. J. (1978). Equal employment opportunity issues in training. *Human Factors, 20*(2), 179-188.

Basarab, Sr., D. J. (1990). Calculating the return on training investment. *Evaluation Practice, 11*(3), 177-185.

Beatty, R. W., & Schneier, C. E. (1977). *Personnel administration: An experiential skills-building approach.* Reading, MA: Addison-Wesley.

Beer, M. (1980). *Organization change and development: A system's view.* Santa Monica, CA: Goodyear.

Benjamin, S. (1989). A closer look at needs analysis and needs assessment: Whatever happened to the system's approach? *Performance and Instruction, 28*(9), 12-16.

Benson, J., & Clark, F. (1982). A guide for instrument development and validation. *The American Journal of Occupational Therapy, 36*(12), 789-800.

Bitner, M. J., Booms, B. H., & Mohr, L. A. (1994). Critical service encounters: The employee's viewpoint. *Journal of Marketing, 58*(1), 95-106.

Blake, R. R., & Mouton, J. S. (1978). *The new managerial grid.* Houston: Gulf.

Bloom, B. S., Engelhart, M. D., Furst, E. J., Hill, W. H., & Krathwohl, D. R. (1956). *Taxonomy of educational objectives: Handbook 1: Cognitive domain.* New York: David McKay.

Blumberg, M., & Pringle, C. D. (1982). The missing opportunity in organizational research: Some implications for a theory of work performance. *Academy of Management Review, 7*(4), 560-569.

Boice, R. (1983). Observational skills. *Psychological Bulletin, 93*(1), 3-29.

Boyatzis, R. E. (1982). *The competent manager: A model for effective performance.* New York: John Wiley and Sons.

Brandt, R. (1981). *Studying behaviors in natural settings.* Lanham, MD: University Press of America.

Brenneman, J. D. (1989). When you can't use a crowd: Single-subject testing. *Performance and Instruction, 28*(3), 22-25.

Brethower, D. M. (1994). Strategic improvement of workplace competence. In P. J. Dean (Ed.), *Performance engineering at work* (pp. 81-106). Batavia, IL: International Board of Standards for Training, Performance and Instruction.

Brewer, J., & Hunter, A. (1989). *Multimethod research: A synthesis of styles.* Newbury Park, CA: Sage.

Brinkerhoff, R. O. (1991). *Achieving results from training.* San Francisco: Jossey-Bass.

Brinkerhoff, R. O., & Gill, S. J. (1994). *The learning alliance: System's thinking in human resources development.* San Francisco: Jossey-Bass.

Brinkerhoff, R. O., & Montesino, M. U. (1995). Partnerships for training transfer: Lessons from a corporate study. *Human Resources Development Quarterly, 6*(3), 263-274.

Brown, I. E., & Davis, P. (1989). Making training meet the needs of the organization: Rehearsal and post-training follow-up sessions to improve success. *Performance and Instruction, 28*(8), 13-16.

Burack, E. H. (1988). *Creative human resource planning and applications: A strategic approach.* Englewood Cliffs, NJ: Prentice Hall.

Burack, E. H., & Mathys, N. J. (1980). *Human resources planning: A pragmatic approach to manpower staffing and development.* Lake Forest, IL: Brace Park.

Burchett, S. R., & De Meuse, K. P. (1985). Performance appraisal and the law. *Personnel, 62*(7), 29-37.

Camp, R. C. (1989). *Benchmarking: The search for industry best practices that lead to superior performance.* Milwaukee, WI: ASQC Quality Press.

Campbell, D. T., & Stanley, J. C. (1963). *Experimental and quasi-experimental designs for research.* Chicago: Rand McNally.

Campbell, J., Dunnette, M., Arvey, R., & Hellervik, L. (1973). The development and evaluation of behaviorally based rating scales. *Journal of Applied Psychology, 57*(1), 15-22.

Canter, J. A. (1987). Developing multiple choice test items. *Training and Development Journal, 41*(5), 85-88.

Cascio, W. F. (1982). *Costing human resources: The financial impact of behavior in organizations.* New York: Van Nostrand Reinhold.

Chelimsky, E. (1985). Comparing and contrasting auditing and evaluation. *Evaluation Review, 9*(4), 483-503.

Clardy, A. B. (1985). *Leadership for performance excellence.* Columbia, MD: Professional Training Services.

Clardy, A. B. (1994). *50 case studies for management and supervisory training.* Amherst, MA: HRD Press.

Clardy, A. B. (1996). *Managing human resources, exercises, experiments and applications workbook.* Mahwah, NJ: LEA Press.

Clark, R. E. (1992). How the cognitive sciences are shaping the profession. In H. D. Stolovitch & E. J. Keeps (Eds.), *Handbook of human performance technology* (pp. 688-700). San Francisco: Jossey-Bass.

Coleman, M. E. (1992). Developing skills and enhancing professional competence. In H. D. Stolovitch & E. J. Keeps, (Eds.), *Handbook of human performance technology* (pp. 634-648). San Francisco: Jossey-Bass.

Conner, R., Jacobi, M., Altman, D., & Aslanian, C. (1985). Measuring need and demands in evaluation research. *Evaluation Review, 9*(6), 717-734.

Cook, T., & Campbell, D. T. (1979). *Quasi-experimentation: Design and analysis issues for field settings.* Boston: Houghton Mifflin.

Copley, P. O., Roubinek, D. G., Layton, J. R., Range, D. G., & McNinch, G. (1982). Implementing and evaluating reading. In C. Klevins (Ed.), *Materials and methods in adult and continuing education* (pp. 155-170). Los Angeles: Klevens.

Crocker, L., & Algina, J. (1986). *Introduction to classical and modern test theory.* New York: Holt, Rinehart & Winston.

Dean, P. J. (Ed.). (1994). *Performance engineering at work.* Batavia, IL: International Board of Standards for Training, Performance and Instruction.

Delbecq, A. L., Van de Ven, A. H., & Gustafson, D. H. (1975). *Group techniques for program planning.* Glenview, IL: Scott Foresman.

Denova, C. C. (1979). *Test construction for training evaluation.* Madison, WI: ASTD.

DeVellis, R. F. (1991). *Scale development, theory and applications.* Newbury Park, CA: Sage.

Dormant, D. (1992). Implementing human performance technology in organizations. In H. D. Stolovitch & E. J. Keeps (Eds.), *Handbook of human performance technology* (pp. 167-187). San Francisco: Jossey-Bass.

Doughty, P. L., & Stakenas, R. (1973). An analysis of costs and effectiveness of an individualized subject offering. In C. D. Sabine (Ed.), *Accountability: Systems planning in education* (pp. 165-191). Homewood, IL: ETC.

Downs, S. (1985). *Testing trainability.* Philadelphia: NFER-Nelson.

Drury, C. G. (1990). Methods for direct observation of performance. In J. R. Wilson & E. N. Corlett, (Eds.), *Evaluation of human work: A practical ergonomics methodology* (2nd ed.) (pp. 45-68). London: Taylor and Francis.

Dun and Bradstreet Information Services. (1995). *Industry norms and key business ratios, Desk top edition.* New York: Author.

Dunnette, M. D., & Kirchner, W. K. (1951). A checklist for differentiating different kinds of sales jobs. *Personnel Psychology, 12*(3), 421-430.

Dweck, C. S. (1986). Motivational processes affecting learning. *American Psychologist, 41*(10), 1040-1048.

Egan, G. (1982). *The skilled helper model, skills, and methods for effective helping* (2nd. ed.). Monterey, CA: Brooks/Cole.

Erickson, P. R. (1990). Evaluating training results. *Training & Development, 44*(1), 57-59.

Fay, C. H. (1990). Performance management as a strategy to increase productivity. *Compensation and Benefits Management, 6*(4), 346-353.

Fiedler, F. E., Chemers, M. M., & Mahar, L. (1977). *Improving leadership effectiveness: The leader match concept.* New York: John Wiley and Sons.

Fitz-enz, J. (1993). How to make benchmarking work for you. *HR Magazine, 38*(12), 40-50.

Ford, D. J. (1993). Benchmarking HRD. *Training & Development, 47*(6), 37-41.

Fowler, Jr., F. J. (1984). *Survey research methods.* Beverly Hills, CA: Sage.

Fowler, Jr., F. J., & Mangione, T. W. (1990). *Standardized survey interviewing: Minimizing interviewer-related error*. Newbury Park, CA: Sage.

Gael, S. (1983). *Job analysis*. San Francisco: Jossey-Bass.

Gagne, R. M., Briggs, L. J., & Wager, W. W. (1988). *Principles of instructional design* (3rd ed.). New York: Holt, Rinehart & Winston.

Geis, G. L. (1987). Formative evaluation: Developmental testing and expert review. *Performance and Instruction, 26*(4), 1-8.

Gilbert, T. F. (1978). *Human competence: Engineering worthy performance*. New York: McGraw Hill.

Gilbert, T. F. (1982). A question of performance part I: The PROBE model. *Training & Development, 36*(9), 20-30.

Glickman, A., & Vallance, T. R. (1958). Curriculum assessment with critical incidents. *Journal of Applied Psychology, 42*(5), 329-335.

Goldstein, I. L. (1986). *Training in organizations: Needs assessment, development and evaluation* (2nd ed.). Monterey, CA: Brooks Cole.

Goldstein, J. (1989, Spring). The affirmative core of resistance to change. *Organization Development Journal*, 32-38.

Gordon, R. (1992). What do instructional designers actually do? An initial investigation of expert practice. *Performance Improvement Quarterly, 5*(2), 65-86.

Graziano, A. M., & Raulin, M. L. (1993). *Research methods: A process of inquiry* (2nd ed.). New York: HarperCollins.

Greene, J., & McClintock, C. (1985). Triangulation in evaluation: Design and analysis issues. *Evaluation Review, 9*(5), 523-545.

Guba, E. G., & Lincoln, Y. S. (1981). *Effective evaluation*. San Francisco: Jossey-Bass.

Guglielmino, L., Long, D., & Mrowicki, L. (n.d.). *Basic skills needs analysis and curriculum design for the work place*. Tallahasee, FL: Workforce Literacy Cooperative Training and Dissemination Project.

Guilford, J. P. (1954). *Psychometric methods*. New York: McGraw Hill.

Haccoun, R. R., & Hamtiaux, T. (1994). Optimizing knowledge tests for inferring learning acquisition levels in single group training evaluation designs: The internal referencing strategy. *Personnel Psychology, 47*(3), 593-604.

Hall, G. E., Loucks, S. F., Rutherford, W. L., & Newlove, B. W. (1975). Levels of use of the innovation: A framework for analyzing innovation adoption. *Journal of Teacher Education, 26*(1), 52-56.

Harrison, E. L., Pietri, P. H., & Moore, C. C. (1983). How to use nominal group technique to assess training needs. *Training, 20*(3), 30-34.

Harrison, M. I. (1994). *Diagnosing organizations: Methods, models and processes* (2nd ed.). Thousand Oaks, CA: Sage.

Harvey, D. F., & Brown, D. R. (1976). *An experiential approach to organization development*. Englewood Cliffs, NJ: Prentice Hall.

Higgins, N. C. (1986). Occupational stress and working women: The effectiveness of two stress reduction programs. *Journal of Vocational Behavior, 29*(1), 66-78.

Hills, F. S., & Bergmann, T. J. (1987). Conducting an 'equal pay for equal work' audit. In D. B. Balking & L. R. Gomez Mejia (Eds.), *New perspectives on compensation* (pp. 80-92). Englewood Cliffs, NJ: Prentice Hall.

Holton, III, E. F. (1996). The flawed four-level evaluation model. *Human Resources Development Quarterly, 7*(1), 2-21.

Hunter, M. (1971). *Teach for transfer: A programmed book*. El Segundo, CA: TIP.

James, B. (1956). Can "needs" define educational goals? *Adult Education, 7*(1), 19-26.

Jelsma, O., Van Merrienboer, J. J., & Bijlstra, J. P. (1990). The ADAPT design model: Towards instructional control of transfer. *Instructional Science, 19,* 89-120.

Johnson, R. (1996). 401(k) training: A delicate balance. *Training, 33*(3), 58-63.

Kaufman, R., & Keller, J. M. (1994). Levels of evaluation: Beyond Kirkpatrick. *Human Resources Development Quarterly, 5*(4), 371-380.

Kaufman, R., & Thomas, S. (1980). *Evaluation without fear.* New York: New Viewpoints.

Kaufman, R., & Valentine, G. (1989). Relating needs assessment and needs analysis. *Performance and Instruction, 28*(10), 10-14.

Kearsley, G. (1982). *Costs, benefits, and productivity in training systems.* Reading, MA: Addison-Wesley.

Keil, E. C. (1981). *Assessment centers: A guide for human resources management.* Reading, MA: Addison-Wesley.

Keller, J. M. (1979). Motivation and instructional design: A theoretical perspective. *Journal of Instructional Development, 2*(4), 26-34.

Keller, J. M. (1983). Motivational design of instruction. In C. M. Reigeluth (Ed.), *Instructional design theories and models: An overview of their current status* (pp. 383-434). Hillsdale, NJ: Erlbaum.

Kelly, P. (1993). Conduct a glass ceiling self-audit now. *HRMagazine, 38*(10), 76-80.

Kerlinger, F. N. (1973). *Foundations of behavioral research* (2nd ed.). New York: Holt, Rinehart & Winston.

King, J. A., Morris, L. L., & Fitzgibbon, C. T. (1987). *How to assess program implementation.* Newbury Park, CA: Sage.

Kirk, J., & Miller, M. L. (1986). *Reliability and validity in qualitative research.* Newbury Park, CA: Sage.

Kirkpatrick, D. (1987). Evaluation. In R. Craig (Ed.), *Training and development handbook: A guide to human resource development* (3rd ed.) (pp. 294-312). New York: McGraw Hill.

Kirkpatrick, D. L. (1994). *Evaluating training programs: The four levels.* San Francisco: Berrett-Koehler.

Kirsch, I. S., Jungeblut, A., Jenkins, L., & Kolstad, A. (1993). *Adult literacy in America.* Washington, DC: U.S. Department of Education, Office of Educational Research and Improvement.

Kling, J. (1995). High performance work systems and firm performance. *Monthly Labor Review, 118*(5), 29-36.

Kolb, D. A., Osland, J. S., & Rubin, I. M. (1995). *Organizational behavior: An experiential approach.* Englewood Cliffs, NJ: Prentice Hall.

Komaki, J. L. (1982). The case for the single case: Making judicious decisions about alternatives. In L. W. Frederiksen (Ed.), *Handbook of organizational behavior management* (pp. 145-176). New York: John Wiley and Sons.

Kraiger, K., Ford, J. K., & Salas, E. (1993). Application of cognitive, skill-based and affective theories of learning outcomes to new methods of training evaluation. *Journal of Applied Psychology, 78*(2), 311-328.

Krathwohl, D. R. (1985). *Social and behavioral science research.* San Francisco: Jossey-Bass.

Krathwohl, D. R., Bloom, B. S., & Masia, B. B. (1964). *Taxonomy of educational objectives, handbook II: Affective domain.* New York: David McKay.

Kreuger, R. (1988). *Focus groups: A practical guide for applied research.* Newbury Park, CA: Sage.

Krusemark, D. M. (1990). *Workplace learning: Preparing the workers of today for the workplace of tomorrow.* New York: New York State AFL-CIO.

Kutner, M. A., Sherman, R. Z., Webb, L., & Fisher, C. J. (1991). *A review of the National Workplace Literacy Program.* Washington, DC: U.S. Department of Education.

Larson, C. E., & LaFasto, F. M. (1989). *Teamwork: What must go right/what can go wrong.* Newbury Park, CA: Sage.

Ledvinka, J., & Scarpello, V. G. (1992). *Federal regulation of personnel and human resource management.* Belmont, CA: Wadsworth.

Lewis, J. B. (1992). *Employment practices loss prevention guidelines.* Warren, NJ: Chubb Group of Insurance Companies.

Linstone, H. A. (1978). The Delphi Technique. In J. Fowles (Ed.), *Handbook of futures research* (pp. 273-300). Westport, CT: Greenwood.

Locke, E., & Latham, G. (1990). *A theory of goal setting and task performance.* Englewood Cliffs, NJ: Prentice Hall.

London, M., & Beatty, R. W. (1993). 360-degree feedback as a competitive advantage. *Human Resource Management, 32*(2 & 3), 353-372.

Mager, R. F. (1968). *Developing attitudes towards learning.* Belmont, CA: Fearon Pitman.

Mager, R. F. (1972). *Goal analysis.* Belmont, CA: Fearon Pitman.

Mager, R. F., & Pipe, P. (1970). *Analyzing performance problems, or "You really oughta wanna."* Belmont, CA: Fearon Pitman.

Main, J. (1992, October 19). How to steal the best ideas around. *Fortune,* pp. 102-106.

Manly, D., Mullarkey, J. E., Bentley, C., Cardona, P., Flesch, L., & Suyams, B. (1991). *Workplace educational skills analysis training guide.* Madison, WI: Wisconsin Board of Vocational, Technical and Adult Education.

Marbella, J. (1994, October 4). Running the gauntlet. *The Baltimore Sun,* pp. D1, D6.

Mark, M. (1983). Treatment implementation, statistical power and internal validity. *Evaluation Review, 7*(4), 543-549.

Mathiason, G. G., & Pierce, N. A. (1996, September-October). Hidden training requirements can create liabilities. *Corporate University Review,* 26-27.

Mattimore-Knudson, R. (1983). The concept of need: Its hedonistic and logical nature. *Adult Education, 33*(2), 117-124.

Maurer, T. J., & Alexander, R. A. (1992). Methods of improving employment test critical scores derived by judging test content: Review and critique. *Personnel Psychology, 45*(4), 727-762.

McCormick, E. J. (1976). Job and task analysis. In M. D. Dunnette (Ed.), *Handbook of industrial and organizational psychology* (pp. 651-696). Chicago: Rand McNally.

McCrossan, L. V., & Garrett, C. D. (1992). *Reading, writing and critical thinking for second-level employees in small and mid-sized businesses.* Allentown, PA: Adult Literacy Center of the Lehigh Valley.

McDonald, F. J. (1987). Strategic evaluation of training. In L. S. May, C. A. Moore, & S. J. Zammit (Eds.), *Evaluating business and industry training* (pp. 19-40). Boston: Kluwer.

McEnery, J., & McEnery, J. M. (1987). Self rating in management training needs assessment: A neglected opportunity. *Journal of Occupational Psychology, 60*(1), 49-60.

Mezoff, B. (1981). How to get accurate self-reports of training outcomes. *Training & Development, 35*(9), 56-61.

Mezoff, B. (1983). Six more benefits of pretesting trainees. *Training, 20*(8), 45-47.

Miles, M. B., & Huberman, A. M. (1984). *Qualitative data analysis.* Newbury Park, CA: Sage.

Miller, A., & Abramson, P. (1987, May 4). Corporate mind control. *Newsweek,* 38-39.

Miller, R. B., Heiman, S. E., & Tuleja, T. (1985). *Strategic selling.* New York: Warner.

Mirabile, R., Caldwell, D., & O'Reilly, C. (1987). Soft skills, hard numbers. *Training, 24*(8), 53-56.

Mitchell, E. J., & Hyde, A. C. (1979). Training demand assessment: Three case studies in planning training programs. *Public Personnel Management, 8*(6), 360-373.

Montebello, A. R., & Haga, M. (1994). To justify training, test, test again. *Personnel Journal, 73*(1), 83-87.

Morris, L. L., Fitzgibbon, C., & Lindheim, E. (1987a). *How to measure attitudes.* Newbury Park, CA: Sage.

Morris, L. L., Fitzgibbon, C., & Lindheim, E. (1987b). *How to measure performance and use tests.* Newbury Park, CA: Sage.

Muchinsky, P. M. (1975, April). Utility of work samples. *Personnel Journal, 54*(4), 218-220.

Murphy, S. (1987). Mirroring instructional technique: A process evaluation model. *Training and Development Journal, 41*(6), 104-107.

Myers-Goodman, J. (1990). Auditing the data in the HRIS. *Personnel, 67*(8), 10-13.

Nadler, L. (1982). *Designing training programs: The critical events model.* Reading, MA: Addison-Wesley.

National Research Council. (1991). *In the mind's eye: Enhancing human performance.* Washington, DC: National Academy Press.

Nevo, D. (1983). The conceptualization of educational evaluation: An analytical review of the literature. *Review of Educational Research, 53*(1), 117-128.

Newstrom, J. W. (1987). Confronting anomalies in evaluation. *Training & Development, 41*(7), 58-60.

Newstrom, J. W., & Lengnick-Hall, M. L. (1991). One size does not fit all. *Training & Development, 45*(6), 43-47.

Nielsen, L. A., & Turner, S. D. (1985). Measuring outcomes of in-service training programs. *Evaluation Review, 9*(6), 751-771.

1995 industry report: Training budgets. (1995). *Training Magazine, 32*(10), 41-48.

Nowack, K. M. (1991). A true training needs analysis. *Training & Development, 45*(4), 69-73.

Olshfski, D., & Joseph, A. (1991). Assessing training needs of executives using the Delphi technique. *Public Productivity and Management Review, 14*(3), 297-301.

OSHA. (1991). *Hazard communication guidelines for compliance* (No. 3111). Washington, DC: U.S. Department of Labor.

OSHA. (1992a). *Chemical hazard communication* (No. 3084). Washington, DC: U.S. Department of Labor.

OSHA. (1992b). *Training requirements in OSHA: Standards and guidelines* (No. 2254). Washington, DC: U.S. Department of Labor.

Ostroff, C., & Ford, J. K. (1989). Assessing training needs: Critical levels of analysis. In I. L. Goldstein (Ed.), *Training and development in organizations* (pp. 25-62). San Francisco: Jossey-Bass.

Owenby, P. H. (1992). Making case studies come alive. *Training, 29*(1), 43-46.

Panell, R., & Laabs, G. (1979). Construction of a criterion-referenced, diagnostic test for an individualized instruction program. *Journal of Applied Psychology, 64*(3), 255-261.

Parry, S. B. (1996). The quest for competencies. *Training, 33*(7), 48-56.

Patton, M. Q. (1980). *Qualitative evaluation methods.* Beverly Hills, CA: Sage.

Peak, H. (1965). Problems of objective observation. In L. Festinger & D. Katz (Eds.), *Research methods in the behavioral sciences* (2nd ed.) (pp. 243-299). New York: Dryden.

Peters, L. H., O'Connor, E. J., & Rudolf, C. J. (1980). The behavioral and affective consequences of performance-relevant situational variables. *Organizational Behavior and Human Performance, 25*(1), 79-96.

Pfeffer, J. (1994). *Competitive advantage through people.* Boston: Harvard Business School Press.

Pine, J., & Tingley, J. C. (1993). ROI of soft-skills training. *Training, 30*(2), 55-60.

Piskurich, G. M. (1993). *Self-directed learning: A practical guide to design, development and implementation.* San Francisco: Jossey-Bass.

Popham, W. J. (1975). *Educational evaluation.* Englewood Cliffs, NJ: Prentice Hall.

Pregnancy discrimination. (1995, January). *Human Resource Manager's Legal Reporter, 305,* 1-2.

Provus, M. (1971). *Discrepancy evaluation for educational program improvement and assessment.* Berkeley, CA: McCutchan.

Rackman, N., & Ruff, R. (1991). *Managing major sales: Practical strategies for improving sales effectiveness.* New York: HarperBusiness.

Rackman, N. (1988). *SPIN selling.* New York: McGraw Hill.

Roethlisberger, F. J., & Dickson, W. J. (1950). *Management and the worker.* Cambridge, MA: Harvard University Press.

Rosenberg, M. J. (1990). Performance technology, working the system. *Training, 27*(2), 42-48.

Rosenberg, M. J., & Smitley, W. (1983). Constructing tests that work. *Training, 20*(9), 41-48.

Rosinger, G., Myers, L. B., Levy, G. W., Loar, M., Mohrman, S. A., & Stock, J. R. (1982). Development of a behavior ally based performance appraisal system. *Personnel Psychology, 35*(1), 75-88.

Rossett, A. (1990). Overcoming obstacles to needs assessment. *Training, 27*(3), 36-41.

Rossi, P. H., & Freeman, H. E. (1993). *Evaluation: A systematic approach.* Newbury Park, CA: Sage.

Rothwell, W. J., & Brandenburg, D. C. (1990). *The workplace literacy primer: An action manual for training and development professionals.* Amherst, MA: HRD.

Rothwell, W. J., & Kazanas, H. C. (1989). *Strategic human resource development.* Englewood Cliffs, NJ: Prentice Hall.

Rothwell, W. J., & Kazanas, H. C. (1992). *Mastering the instructional design process.* San Francisco: Jossey-Bass.

Rowland, G. (1992). What do instructional designers actually do? An initial investigation of expert practices. *Performance Improvement Quarterly, 5*(2), 65-86.

Rubin, H. J., & Rubin, I. S. (1995). *Qualitative interviewing: The art of hearing data.* Thousand Oaks, CA: Sage.

Rummler, G. A., & Brache, A. P. (1990). *Improving performance: How to manage the white space on the organization chart.* San Francisco: Jossey-Bass.

Rummler, G. A., & Brache, A. P. (1992). Transforming organizations through human performance technology. In H. D. Stolovitch & E. J. Keeps (Eds.), *Handbook of human performance technology* (pp. 32-49). San Francisco: Jossey-Bass.

Sackett, P. R., & Mullen, E. J. (1993). Beyond formal experimental design: Towards an expanded view of the training evaluation process. *Personnel Psychology, 46*(3), 613-627.

Salinger, R. D. (1973). *Disincentives to effective employee training and development.* Washington, DC: U.S. Civil Service Commission.

Salinger, R. D. (1979). Measuring behavioral change which results from training. In R. O. Peterson (Ed.), *Determining the payoff of management training* (pp. 113-150). Madison, WI: ASTD.

Sanders, P., & Yanouzas, J. N. (1983). Socialization to learning. *Training & Development, 37*(7), 14-21.

Scheirer, M. A., & Rezmovic, E. L. (1983). Measuring the degree of program implementation: A methodological review. *Evaluation Review, 7*(5), 599-633.

Schmitt, B. Gulliland, S. W., Landis, R. S., & Devine, D. (1993). Computer-based testing applied to selection of secretarial applicants. *Personnel Psychology, 46*(1), 149-165.

Schneider, B., & Konz, A. M. (1989). Strategic job analysis. *Human Resources Management, 28*(1), 51-63.

Schneier, C. E., & Johnson, C. (1993). Benchmarking: A tool for improving performance management and reward system. *ACA Journal, 2*(1), 14-31.

Schneier, C. E., Guthrie, J. P., & Olian, J. D. (1988). A practical approach to conducting and using training needs assessment. *Public Personnel Management, 17*(2), 191-205.

Schonberg, G. (1993). *Flex: A flexible tool for continuously improving your evaluation of training effectiveness.* Amherst, MA: HRD.

Scissons, E. (1982). A typology of needs assessment definitions in adult education. *Adult Education, 33*(1), 20-28.

Scriven, M. (1973a). The methodology of evaluation. In B. R. Worthen & J. B. Sanders (Eds.), *Educational evaluation: Theory and practice* (pp. 60-106). Worthington, OH.: Charles Jones.

Scriven, M. (1973b). Goal free evaluation. In E. R. House (Ed.), *School evaluation: The politics and process* (pp. 319-331). Berkeley, CA: McCutchan.

Seegers, J. J. J. L. (1989). Assessment centers for identifying long-term potential and for self-development. In P. Herriot (Ed.), *Assessment and selection in organizations* (pp. 745-771). Chichester, UK: Wiley and Sons.

Selltiz, C., Jahoda, M., Deutsch, M., & Cook, S. W. (1964). *Research methods in social relations* (Rev. ed.). New York: Holt, Rinehart & Winston.

Shore, B. A., Lerman, D. C., Smith, R. G., Iwata, B. A., & DeLeon, I. G. (1995). Direct assessment of quality of care in a geriatric nursing home. *Journal of Applied Behavioral Analysis, 28*(4), 435-448.

Shrock, S., Mansukham, R. M., Coscarelli, W., & Palmer, S. (1986). An overview of criterion-referenced test development. *Performance and Instruction Journal, 25*(6), 3-7.

Smith, B., Delahaye, B., & Gates, P. (1986). Some observations on TNA. *Training & Development, 40*(8), 63-68.

Smith, P., & Kendall, L. M. (1963). Retranslation of expectations: An approach to the construction of unambiguous anchors for rating scales. *Journal of Applied Psychology, 47*(2), 149-155.

Spencer, L. M. (1986). *Calculating human resource costs and benefits.* New York: John Wiley and Sons.

Sproul, L. S. (1986). Using electronic mail for data collection in organization research. *Academy of Management Journal, 29*(1), 159-169.

Steadman, S. V. (1980). Learning to select a needs assessment strategy. *Training & Development, 34*(1), 56-61.

Steecher, B. M., & Davis, W. A. (1987). *How to focus an evaluation.* Newbury Park, CA: Sage.

Stewart, D. W., & Kamins, M. A. (1993). *Secondary research: Information sources and methods* (2nd. ed.). Newbury Park, CA: Sage.

Stolovitch, H. D. (1978). The intermediate technology of learner verification and revision. *Educational Technology, 18*(2), 13-17.

Stufflebeam, D. L., Foley, W. J., Gephart, W. J., Guba, E. G., Hammond, R. L., Merriman, H. O., & Provus, M. M. (1971). *Educational evaluation and decision-making.* Itasca, IL: F. E. Peacock.

Swanson, R. A., & Gradous, D. B. (1988). *Forecasting financial benefits of human resource development.* San Francisco: Jossey-Bass.

Sweetland, R. C., & Keyser, D. J. (Eds.). (1991). *Tests: A comprehensive reference for assessments in psychology, education and business.* Austin, TX: Pro-Ed.

Talley, R. A. (1986). A new methodology for evaluating the curricular relevancy of police academy training. *Journal of Police Science and Administration, 14*(2), 112-120.

Tannenbaum, R., Marguiles, N., Massarik, F., & Associates. (Eds.). (1987). *Human systems development.* San Francisco: Jossey-Bass.

Thornton, III, G. C., & Byham, W. C. (1982). *Assessment centers and managerial performance.* New York: Academic Press.

Tompkins, N. C. (1993). Conduct constructive safety audits. *HRMagazine, 38*(7), 55-56.

Trimby, M. J. (1979). Needs assessment models: A comparison. *Educational Technology, 19*(12), 24-28.

Tyler, R. W. (1942). General statement on evaluation. *Journal of Educational Research, 35*(7), 492-501.

U.S. Department of Education. (1988). *The bottom line: Basic skills in the workplace.* Washington, DC: Government Printing Office.

U.S. Department of Labor. (1991). *Office of Federal Contract Programs compliance manual* (029-016-00148-4). Washington, DC: Government Printing Office.

Walker, J. (1980). *Human resources planning.* New York: McGraw Hill.

Wallace, W. (1991). *Auditing* (2nd ed.). Boston: KWS-Kent.

Warrenfeltz, R. B. (1989). An achievement based approach to evaluating engineering technicians. *Public Personnel Management, 18*(3), 243-262.

Weisbord, M. R. (1987). *Productive workplaces.* San Francisco: Jossey-Bass.

Wellins, R. S., Byham, W. C., & Wilson, J. M. (1991). *Empowered teams.* San Francisco: Jossey-Bass.

Wiesen, J. P. (1987). Use of training data in personnel decision-making. In L. S. May, C. A. Moore, & S. J. Zammit (Eds.), *Evaluating business and industry training* (pp. 265-284). Boston: Kluwer.

Williams, J. M. (1972). Questionnaire design. In R. Worcester (Ed.), *Consumer market research handbook* (pp. 69-102). London: McGraw Hill.

Wilson, J. R., & Corlett, E. N. (Eds.). (1990). *Evaluation of human work* (2nd ed.). London: Taylor and Francis.

Witkin, R. B. (1984). *Assessing needs in educational and social programs.* San Francisco: Jossey-Bass.

Wlodkowski, R. J. (1988). *Enhancing adult motivation to learn.* San Francisco: Jossey-Bass.

Woolsey, L. K. (1986). The critical incident technique: An innovative qualitative method of research. *Canadian Journal of Counseling, 20*(4), 242-254.

Worthen, B. R. (1977). Characteristics of good evaluation studies. *Journal of Research and Development in Education, 10*(3), 3-20.

Yelon, S. L. (1992). Classroom instruction. In H. D. Stolovitch & E. J. Keeps (Eds.), *Handbook of human performance technology* (pp. 383-411). San Francisco: Jossey-Bass.

Yin, R. K. (1989). *Case study research: Design and methods.* Newbury Park, CA: Sage.

Zeira, Y., & Avedisian, J. (1989). Organizational planned change: Assessing the chances for success. *Organization Dynamics, 17*(4), 31-45.

Zemke, R., & Kramlinger, T. (1982). *Figuring things out: A trainer's guide to needs and task analysis.* Reading, MA: Addison-Wesley.

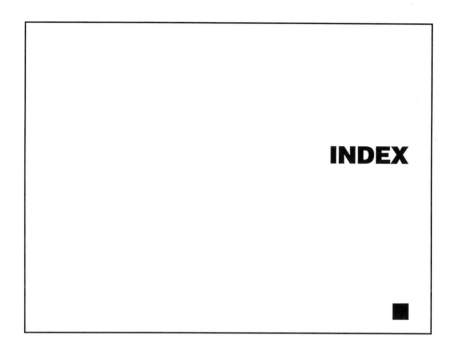

INDEX

ABOUT THE AUTHOR

■

Alan Clardy completed his PhD from the University of Maryland College Park with a concentration in training and adult education. He has worked in the fields of human resources management and development for more than 20 years. He started and managed a training department for a major Baltimore bank before beginning a private practice in human resources consulting. He also served as Vice President of Human Resources. He currently is the principal for Advantage Human Resources, a consulting firm that specializes in performance management and appraisal, sales and service quality, management development, and human resources management programs.

Dr. Clardy has taught in the graduate programs at Towson State University and Hood College, and has been an adjunct member of the Johns Hopkins University faculty since 1992. He has previously published three voumes, *50 Case Studies for Management and Supervisory Training, Human Resources Management: Exercises, Experiments and Applications, and The NAHB Personnel Workbook.* In addition, he has developed and produced various training and development programs.

.